# THE MARTHA WAY

# The Martha Way

*Essential Principles for Mastering Home and Living*

## MARTHA STEWART

HARVEST

*An Imprint of* WILLIAM MORROW

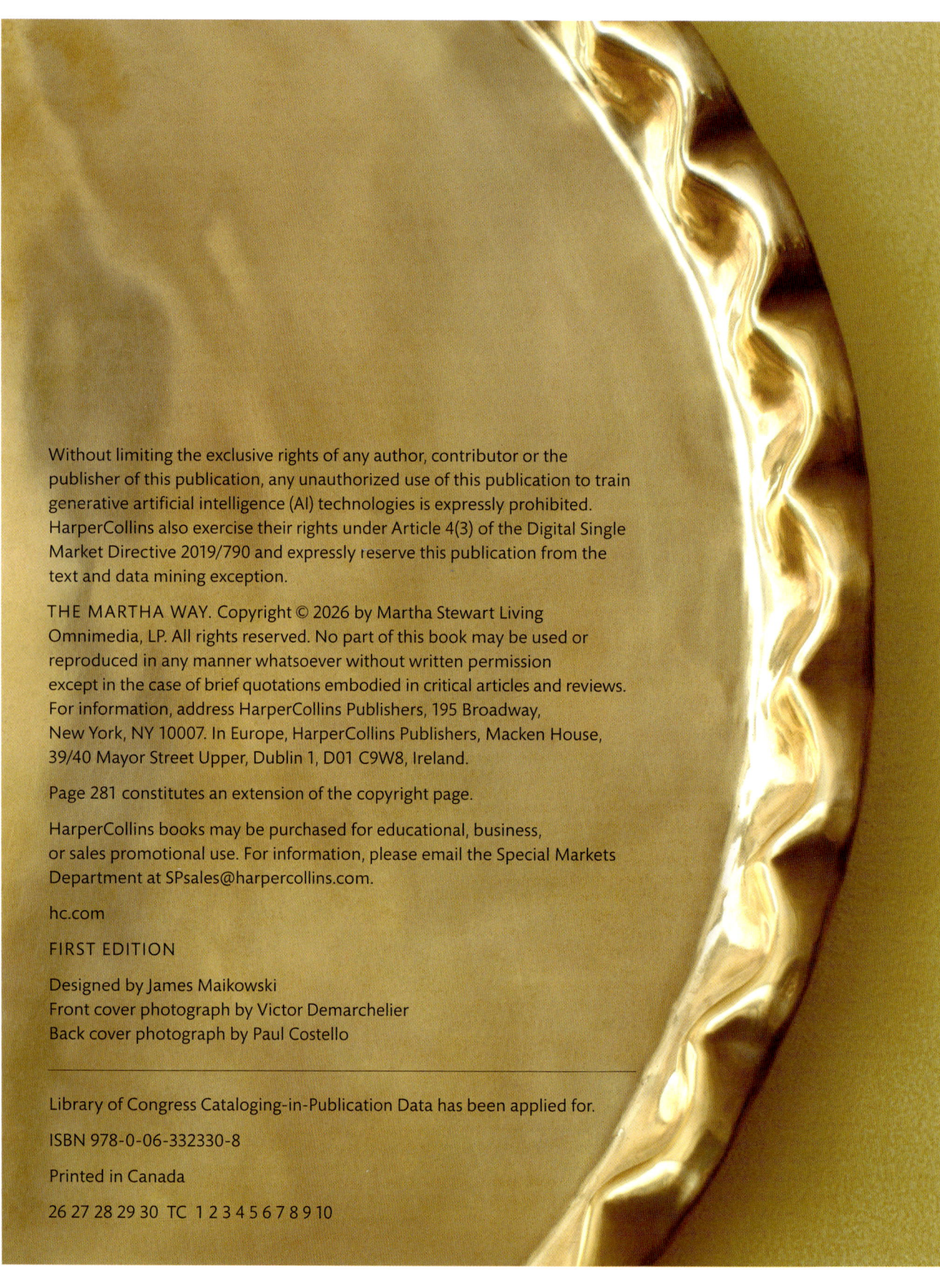

Page 281 constitutes an extension of the copyright page.

HarperCollins books may be purchased for educational, business, or sales promotional use. For information, please email the Special Markets Department at SPsales@harpercollins.com.

hc.com

FIRST EDITION

Designed by James Maikowski
Front cover photograph by Victor Demarchelier
Back cover photograph by Paul Costello

Library of Congress Cataloging-in-Publication Data has been applied for.

ISBN 978-0-06-332330-8

Printed in Canada

26 27 28 29 30 TC 1 2 3 4 5 6 7 8 9 10

To the many individuals who
have inspired me through
instruction, mentorship, and
guidance in every one
of the core areas I hold central
in the subject of LIVING

# CONTENTS

# Cooking

# Entertaining

# Home Organizing

# Collecting

# Gardening

# Welcome to *The Martha Way.*

This book is designed as a master class in elevating the ordinary into the extraordinary, distilling decades of expertise into clear, actionable principles for a well-curated home and life.

The content is organized into five celebrated areas of everyday living: Cooking, Entertaining, Home Organizing, Collecting, and Gardening. Each chapter breaks down a topic into fundamental lessons, with essential steps to success—blueprints you can follow to achieve reliable, aspirational results.

I chose to concentrate on these subject areas—always the focus of my magazines and television shows—because they bring life value and purpose. They grew out of years spent cooking for family and friends, hosting parties big and small, organizing and maintaining homes that had to work as hard as I did, collecting objects (and enjoying them every day), and tending my gardens. I have tested and refined every lesson in each section over my lifetime. Together, they form a cohesive approach to a well-made life—one shaped by intention, discipline, and an abiding respect for quality in all things.

Here's how to make the most of this concise guide:

▸ **Read sequentially and then focus on specific sections as needed.** Take your time reading through the book; then return to the chapters that speak to your immediate interests or challenges—whether it's Home Organizing to help you declutter and customize storage, or Cooking to master specific techniques. Over time, explore all sections, as the principles often interconnect (a thriving vegetable garden supports cooking and entertaining, as does a prized collection of, say, cake stands or glassware, which are displayed best in an orderly environment).

▶ **Focus on the lessons first.** Each chapter opens with foundational philosophies—the "why" behind the methods. These timeless ideas provide the mindset for long-term success.

▶ **Follow the steps to success.** The heart of every chapter is a sequence of achievable steps. Treat them as a roadmap: Master the basics before moving onto more advanced techniques. Practice one step at a time, building habits that become second nature.

▶ **Incorporate the principles.** Look for recurring advice on daily, weekly, seasonal, and annual tasks—such as home cleaning or maintenance calendars. Use a planner or homekeeping log to track your progress, stay proactive, and celebrate small accomplishments along the way.

▶ **Make it personal.** My approach has always emphasized quality, seasonality, and intentionality. Adapt these steps to your space, budget, and passions—whether curating a small collection of cherished items or hosting a gathering.

▶ **Use the book as a lifelong reference.** Return to it seasonally (align garden tasks with the time of year) or whenever inspiration strikes. Remember, steady progress is more important than perfection, and revisiting this guide will support your ongoing success toward a more beautiful, functional, and joyful life.

There's only one way to master the art of everyday living—and it's the Martha Way: thoughtful, precise, and always rewarding.

# COOKING

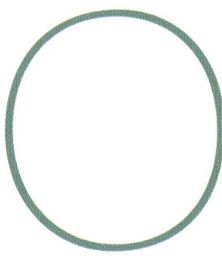

Of the five chapters in this book, cooking and gardening stand out because they require the most in the way of formal education, including serious how-to instruction and lots of trial and error. We perhaps practice them almost every day, year-round, and continually derive tremendous benefits and pleasures from them during our lives.

For most of us, cooking has become an everyday task, a necessity that we can evolve easily into an everyday pleasure if we hone our skills, economize our steps of preparation, shop correctly and efficiently, and include others in our efforts and enjoyment. I am always looking for ways to improve my skills, to invent new skills, or try ones that I glimpsed on Instagram or YouTube or TikTok. Changing an ingredient, trying something different, or attempting a more complex technique can make cooking and baking more enjoyable and more fun.

I have been learning to cook for many years, beginning as a little girl watching my mother in the kitchen. Known in our family as Big Martha, my mother believed deeply in doing things properly: choosing the very best ingredients, treating them with respect, and never cutting corners. Those early lessons shaped not only how I cook, but how I think about food.

Although I never attended a formal cooking school, my career has given me access to some of the world's greatest chefs, teachers, and restaurateurs, and I have learned by observing, asking many questions, and cooking alongside them. In Daniel Boulud's kitchen,

I learned how to roast a whole foie gras. In New York's Chinatown, I discovered how to make dim sum. And on my various television shows, I've properly prepared artichokes with Jean-Georges, rolled the freshest sushi with Nobu Matsuhisa, and roasted a perfect chicken with Jacques Pépin.

Along the way, my team and I have written many cookbooks. Some, including *Cooking School* and *Baking Handbook* and even my hundredth, *Martha: The Cookbook*, are comprehensive; others—*Cookies* and *Pies & Tarts*—are more focused. Each one reflects the techniques, tips, and recipes I have gathered over decades, and is intended to help cooks build a dependable recipe repertoire—dishes you return to again and again.

Today, cooking remains one of the great pleasures of my life, along with sharing that passion with others. I always encourage cooks to master classic techniques and basic knife skills—which make preparation more efficient and enjoyable. Knowing how to properly dice an onion is the first flavor-building step in countless dishes. Equally important are good kitchen habits: reading a recipe all the way through, practicing mise en place, and keeping your workspace clean as you go. These disciplines create both consistency and confidence.

For me, cooking is first and foremost about using what is in season. My gardens and greenhouses provide vegetables and fruits year-round, and I try to use as many of them as possible. I encourage you to do the same, whether you grow your own or shop at a local farmstand. Seek out the freshest meats, cheeses, and eggs, always buying from reliable, trusted sources. The same philosophy applies to pantry staples and kitchen tools—purchase the best quality you can afford, a principle I inherited directly from my mother.

Whether you are cooking for yourself or your family or your friends, mastering these lessons is where to start.

# 1
# COOK SEASONALLY

These days, it's all too easy to buy the same fruits and vegetables throughout the year at grocery stores. But that means you miss out on the anticipation—and variety—of eating produce at its peak. I prefer to align my diet with the seasons, as doing so also benefits your health, your wallet, and the environment. You'll be more inclined to purchase produce that is grown locally and harvested when it has reached its full nutritional value and flavor, rather than being harvested too soon and transported across the country or the globe. I've found that these are some of the best ways to help you eat seasonally year-round:

**Learn what's in season at any given time.** The handy guide on page 30 can help you explore different in-season fruits and vegetables across the country. Of course, the seasonal produce available in your area will vary slightly across different regions, depending on local growing conditions and climate fluctuations.

**Shop locally.** Greenmarkets (also known as farmers' markets) and farmstands typically stock in-season selections, whereas food co-ops, specialty grocers, and natural food stores often focus on sustainable sourcing. An increasing number of supermarkets also promote local produce, making it easier than ever to choose fresh options over those shipped from afar. Many have designated organic sections, too, so you can incorporate more of these healthful (non-GMO and pesticide-free) options into your diet.

**Know how to spot produce at its peak.** To choose peak produce, use your senses: Look for vibrant, even color and plumpness; avoid dullness, bruises, and signs of shriveling (minimal blemishes are fine). Smell for a pleasant, sweet, often earthy aroma. Pick items that feel heavy for their size. Firmness varies—many types of produce (e.g., avocados, peaches, mangoes) should be firm but yield slightly to gentle pressure. Avoid rock-hard (underripe) fruits or anything with soft spots (overripe). For melons, tap for a hollow sound.

**Know what continues to ripen after harvest.** These include avocados, bananas, cantaloupes, kiwis, mangoes, papayas, pears, persimmons, stone fruits (apricots, nectarines, peaches, and plums but not cherries), tomatillos, and tomatoes, all of which should be stored at room temperature—never in the refrigerator—and out of direct sunlight. You can also hasten ripening by placing them in a tightly sealed paper bag with an apple or a banana.

**Vary your recipes and techniques.** Appetites wax and wane over the course of the year. Along with rotating in seasonal produce, focus on creating lighter meals, such as salads, chilled soups, simple pasta dishes, and grilled fish and chicken, for the warmer months. During the fall and winter, opt for heartier soups, stews, braises, baked pastas and other casseroles, roasted meats and vegetables, and robust winter greens.

**Preserve peak-of-season produce.** Cooking seasonally need not mean depriving yourself of a healthy, colorful variety during winter, when fresh options are the most limited. Sliced peaches, nectarines, and mangoes (tossed with a bit of lemon juice to prevent discoloration) can be frozen in a single layer on a baking sheet until they are firm, then transferred to resealable bags or containers for 8 to 12 months. Tomatoes can be slow-roasted to soften and remove excess moisture. First, halve cherry and grape tomatoes, and cut bigger tomatoes into uniformly large pieces. Then, toss with a little olive oil and spread them evenly on a baking sheet. Cook at 275°F for a few hours, until wrinkly and beginning to burst. Once cool, you can freeze the pieces or purée them (if you plan to use in making tomato sauce) and store in airtight containers.

# 2

# EQUIP YOUR KITCHEN

In general, you should try to purchase the best-quality equipment within your budget. It is far better to have a few hand-selected, superior-grade knives and pots and pans—preferably those made of stainless steel—than a whole set of cheaper models, which will inevitably require replacing. More advanced cooks will want to add other tools as noted below.

**Begin with five basics.** These items will cover the most common types of cooking: a 2-quart saucepan, an 8-inch nonstick pan (preferably coated with ceramic rather than Teflon) for omelets and other egg dishes, an 11-inch sauté pan (with straight sides), a 10-inch skillet (with sloping sides), and a large stockpot.

**Procure everyday cooking utensils.** Wooden spoons and spatulas are a must; because they absorb odors and flavors, reserve some for sweets and keep the rest for savory preparations. Flexible (heatproof) silicone spatulas are another standby for cooking eggs, melting chocolate, and folding ingredients. Again, have some for sweet versus savory uses. A slotted metal spoon or spatula lets you transfer and drain foods at the same time, while a solid metal spatula is better at flipping everything from burgers to pancakes, as well as lifting cookies after baking. A fine-mesh sieve (one large, for straining, and one small, for dusting) and a colander are other versatile tools.

**Invest in well-made knives.** You can accomplish nearly all cooking tasks with just three essential high-quality knives that are comfortable to use. A chef's knife is the indispensable multitasker for chopping, slicing, and most heavy-duty tasks. A paring knife is ideal for more precise tasks like peeling and coring produce and deveining shrimp. A serrated (aka bread) knife is designed for slicing crusty bread, soft baked goods, and juicy produce (peaches and tomatoes) without compressing them. One with an offset handle allows better control when chopping chocolate or nuts. Any knife should feel good in your hand—test the weight, grip, and how it balances (the bolster, where blade meets handle, helps with this). Choose forged (not stamped) blades when possible for better balance and longevity. High-carbon stainless steel holds an edge well.

> ▸ **MARTHA COOKS**
> Keeping knives razor-sharp is essential, making meal prep easier, faster, and safer (dull blades are more prone to slipping). First, maintain your knives by honing them, running the blade against a honing steel or rod with each use (per the manufacturer's instructions). When they do need sharpening, consider using a whetstone, which allows you to restore the edge of the blade to a high degree of precision. Other options include an electric knife sharpener—which is faster and more convenient, but can wear away at the knife's edge more quickly over time—or taking your knives to a trusted professional once or twice a year.

**Rely on cast-iron skillets.** They're affordable, ovenproof, excellent heat conductors, and, when properly seasoned, naturally nonstick. They also come in a range of sizes. Many people inherit the same ones used by their parents or grandparents.

> **▸ MARTHA COOKS**
> To clean your cast-iron skillet, first line your sink with a wire rack or towels. Gently scrub the skillet using warm, soapy water and a stiff-bristled brush; then rinse. To prevent rust, wipe it thoroughly with a lint-free towel. Finish by rubbing a little cooking oil on the inside of the pan. To reseason it (when the nonstick surface is wearing thin), place the clean, oil-rubbed pan upside down on the top rack in a 450°F to 500°F oven for 1 hour.

**Add specialty equipment.** Choose pieces depending on how often—and on the types of foods—you cook. A heavy-duty roasting pan with a footed wire rack is used for roasting turkey and large cuts of meat. It's preferable to choose one that is shallow, slope-sided, and features wide handles for easy gripping. An enamel-coated Dutch oven with a tight-fitting lid, suitable for use on the stove or in the oven, is ideal for braising and making soups, stews, and tagines. It is also convenient for baking sourdough boules. Balloon whisks and pastry brushes are essential for bakers; ramekins double as vessels for measured ingredients (see mise en place, page 48) and baking dishes for individual servings of soufflés, custards, and other dishes.

**Consider adding a powerful blender and food processor.** These workhorses do more than make smoothies and chop vegetables. They are also convenient for blending dressings, puréeing soups and sauces, and blitzing bread, nuts, and cookies to fine crumbs. A food processor can even be used to make pie and cookie doughs. If storage space is limited, look for combination models.

**Repurpose common tools.** There's no need to buy three (or more) tools when a single one can do multiple jobs. For example, a coffee grinder does more than grind coffee beans; it also pulverizes nuts, stale bread for breadcrumbs, and granulated sugar (for DIY confectioners' sugar). A Microplane (rasp) grater makes fast work of finely grating hard cheeses, whole nutmeg, fresh turmeric or ginger, peeled garlic cloves, and chocolate. And a meat mallet's different surfaces offer a variety of uses: Besides pounding meat into thin cutlets, the flat (smooth) side is for coarsely crushing nuts, seeds, whole spices, crackers, candies, cookies, and chocolate (place these items in a plastic bag to keep them contained). The flat side also works to easily pit olives and release the oils from lemongrass and ginger. The toothed side is for tenderizing meat, poultry, and seafood—and to crack ice cubes (wrapped in kitchen towels) for drinks.

# 3

# BUILD UP YOUR PANTRY

Minimizing trips to the grocery store will save you time, effort, and money. You will also find it easier to make healthier choices if you base your shopping on planned meals for each week. Ingredients are your most important "tools," so prioritize quality over quantity—such as buying fresh, locally grown produce; pasture-raised meat, poultry, and eggs; wild-caught seafood; and artisanal flours and grains—to ensure the best-tasting dishes and help avoid food waste.

**Take inventory of what you already have.** Go through your pantry, refrigerator, and freezer, noting best-by dates and the condition of any perishables. Then, build that week's meals around those items, making a list of items you need to buy, as well as any basic supplies you need to replenish.

**Look for ways to use food scraps.** Produce that is past its prime but not spoiled can still be put to use, as can the trimmings when prepping produce or other items for a recipe. For example, you can use the scraps from celery, carrots, onions, shallots, and garlic to make a flavorful vegetable stock, or even a chicken stock with saved bones from a whole roasted bird. It's also worth freezing the rinds from Parmesan wedges used for grating, as they lend depth of flavor and a welcome umami to soups and stews (when added about 5 minutes before the end of cooking).

> ▶ **MARTHA COOKS**
> After stripping the kernels off a fresh cob of corn, I like to save the cob to make a delicious and quick corn stock for using as a base for summer soups or chowders or in place of other stocks when making risotto. It is also the beginning of a wonderful pasta sauce when thickened with a little roux and enhanced with grated Parmesan.

**Have an open mind.** When shopping, be prepared to swap items on your list with more optimal fruits and vegetables in the produce aisle or at the farmers' market, following the guidance on page 30.

**Focus on fresh.** Produce sold in plastic bags or clamshell containers is often shipped from far away, causing it to lose flavor and nutrients along its journey. Instead, opt for bunches or heads of greens, lettuces, radishes, carrots, celery, and other vegetables. For the same reason, pass by precut or presliced vegetables in favor of whole fruits and vegetables.

**Shop for building blocks.** Experienced home cooks keep a steady supply of foundational ingredients on hand for ease, efficiency, and impromptu meals. These include whole grains, dried beans and legumes, tinned fish, dried pasta, canned tomatoes, nuts and seeds, and flavor-builders (such as oils and vinegars, spices and dried herbs, mustard, tahini, soy sauce or tamari, tomato paste, and low-sodium stocks). Buying dried foods in bulk saves money and reduces packaging waste. Cooking big batches of grains and beans for freezing gives you an even bigger leg up on a busy weekday.

**Personalize your inventory.** You'll be more inclined to prepare meals at home when you incorporate ingredients from your favorite cuisines—whether it's curry powders and pastes from Southeast Asia, Korean specialties like gochujang and gochugaru, za'atar and sumac for Middle Eastern dishes, or harissa, dukkah, and other North African staples. Pay attention to the dishes you eat at a restaurant or while traveling, and then look for any specialty items to use in your own kitchen.

# 4
# LEARN BASIC COOKING SKILLS

Cooking is more than just following a recipe. Understanding the underlying principles and techniques will give you greater confidence in the kitchen, enabling you to adapt recipes, improvise with your own dishes, and create meals with the utmost efficiency and enjoyment. I learned all my greatest lessons from my mother growing up in our kitchen in Nutley, New Jersey. But I never stopped being curious, never stopped asking questions, never stopped learning from every chef I met. Here's what every home cook needs to know.

**Know how to hold a knife.** It might seem inconsequential, but the first lesson in any cooking school class teaches the proper way to handle a knife. Rather than wrapping your entire hand around the handle, most chefs "choke" the handle with their palm, with the thumb and index finger gripping the base of the blade on either side. Give it a try and you'll see how much less effort it takes to maneuver the knife—you'll be able to cut with much more stability and finesse.

**Know how to chop an onion.** Not only is this a foundational step in many savory recipes, but it also allows you to hone your overall knife skills. Begin by halving the onion through the root. With an onion half cut-side down on your cutting board, trim off the stem end. Peel away the skin, then hold the onion with one hand (curling your fingers to shield from the knife) while making lengthwise slits all the way through the onion, keeping the root end intact. The closer the slits, the finer the dice or mince. Next, slice crosswise in the same intervals. Follow the same basic method for dicing or mincing shallots.

> ▸ **MARTHA COOKS**
> Use a separate cutting board for onions and garlic to avoid fruits and other items absorbing their flavors. I chop onions and anything else being cooked on one cutting board and fruits and vegetables being eaten raw on another.

**Know how to mince garlic.** Here's another flavor-building ingredient that home cooks should be able to prep quickly and effortlessly. Remove the desired number of cloves from a garlic head. Cut crosswise to remove the root end of each clove. Place the flat side of your knife blade over the clove, then press down with the heel of your palm to smash. Pop the crushed garlic out of the papery skins. Gather the cloves together on your cutting board. Steadying the tip of the knife with your other hand, rock the blade back and forth over the cloves until they are appropriately minced, gathering the pieces together again and scraping the sides of the blade as you work.

**Know how to prep fresh herbs.** Often herbs are either minced or finely chopped when used to flavor or garnish dishes. Begin by washing and completely drying them. For soft herbs—such as parsley, cilantro, chervil, and tarragon—strip the leaves from the stems (or retain the stems if using cilantro) by slicing the bunch at a 45-degree angle. For woodsy herbs—such as rosemary, thyme, and oregano—pinch the top of the stem and run your thumb and forefinger down against the direction of growth, stripping the leaves off. Gather the leaves in a neat pile on your cutting board and, using the same rocking motion as for garlic, rock the blade back and forth over the pile. You can stop here or gather the pile again and continue chopping for a finer mince. To cut herbs, such as basil, mint, or sage, into chiffonade, roll the whole leaves into tight cylinders. Slice them very thinly crosswise, just once, so as not to bruise the leaves.

**Know how to prep carrots (and parsnips).** Start by peeling the carrot and trimming the ends. For coins, slice the carrot crosswise into ½-inch rounds. To dice, cut the carrot crosswise into even pieces (about 3 inches long); slice each piece in half lengthwise to create a flat side. Turn the carrot onto its flat side and cut it into ¼-inch planks. Stack the planks and cut them into ¼-inch strips. Cut the strips crosswise to create uniform cubes. For julienne (thin strips), cut the carrot crosswise into even pieces (about 3 inches long). Slice a thin piece off one side to create a flat side, then turn it onto that side. Slice the carrot lengthwise into ⅛-inch slices. Stack these slices and cut them into thin matchsticks.

**Know how to peel tomatoes and peaches.** Blanching is the easiest way to remove the skins, such as when using tomatoes in a sauce or peaches in a dessert or salsa. Score an X in the bottom of each fruit, and place in a pot of boiling water for about 30 seconds. Scoop out the fruit; when cool enough to handle, slip off the skins, using a paring knife to remove any stubborn spots. If not peeling, slice or dice tomatoes and peaches with a serrated knife to prevent the fruit from being squished as you work.

**Know how to prep an artichoke.** Squeeze a halved lemon into a bowl of water before you begin. Working with one artichoke at a time, trim off the top quarter with a serrated knife, then snip off the sharp tips from the remaining leaves with kitchen shears. Pull off any smaller leaves from the base and trim the stem flush with the bottom. Submerge in the lemon water to prevent discoloration.

# Seasonal Produce Guide

This handy chart can help you explore peak-of-season produce throughout the year, and you can focus your shopping and meal-planning accordingly. Seasonality varies widely by area due to climate, soil, latitude, and other factors, so always cross-reference local resources for more accurate timing.

| Season | Produce |
| --- | --- |
| ▸ **ALL YEAR** | Apples, beets, cabbage, carrots, chard, collards, garlic, kale, microgreens, mushrooms, onions, potatoes, shallots, sweet potatoes. |
| ▸ **SPRING** | **All Spring:** arugula, bok choy, broccoli, herbs, lettuces, radishes, scallions, spinach, spring onions. **March:** Brussels sprouts, cauliflower, celery root, chestnuts, kohlrabi, leeks, parsnips, pears, romanesco, turnips, winter squash. **April:** asparagus, green garlic, morels, nettles, parsnips, pea shoots, ramps, rhubarb, strawberries, turnips. **May:** asparagus, dandelion greens, garlic scapes, green garlic, morels, nettles, pea shoots, ramps, rhubarb, snap peas, snow peas, sorrel, strawberries. |
| ▸ **SUMMER** | **All Summer:** blueberries, cucumbers, currants, green beans, herbs, kohlrabi, plums, raspberries, scallions, summer squash, tomatoes. **June:** apricots, arugula, cherries, fava beans, gooseberries, lettuces, radishes, shelling peas, snap peas, snow peas, strawberries. **July:** blackberries, cherries, corn, currants, eggplant, gooseberries, ground cherries, leeks, melons, nectarines, okra, peaches, peppers, shelling beans, snap peas, snow peas, strawberries, tomatillos. **August:** blackberries, celery, corn, edamame, eggplant, grapes, leeks, lima beans, melons, nectarines, okra, peaches, peppers, salad greens, shelling beans, tomatillos, winter squash. |
| ▸ **AUTUMN** | **All Autumn:** bok choy, broccoli, cauliflower, celery, ginger, herbs, kohlrabi, leeks, lettuces, pears, turmeric, winter squash. **September:** corn, cucumbers, currants, eggplant, figs, grapes, green beans, melons, okra, pawpaws, peaches, peppers, plums, salad greens, shelling beans, summer squash, tomatillos, tomatoes. **October:** arugula, Brussels sprouts, chestnuts, cucumbers, eggplant, fennel, green beans, kiwi berries, parsnips, peppers, persimmons, plums, quince, romanesco, scallions, shelling beans, spinach, summer squash, tomatillos, tomatoes, turnips. **November:** arugula, Brussels sprouts, chestnuts, fennel, parsnips, persimmons, quince, romanesco, scallions, spinach, turnips. |
| ▸ **WINTER** | **All Winter:** arugula, bok choy, Brussels sprouts, cauliflower, celery root, chestnuts, fennel, garlic, kohlrabi, leeks, lettuces, parsnips, pears, romanesco, spinach, turnips, winter squash. **December:** broccoli, kalettes, quince. **January:** kalettes, radishes. **February:** herbs, radishes, scallions. |

# 5

# MASTER CLASSIC METHODS

These following building blocks are essential to every home chef. Becoming proficient in them will go a long way when cooking for yourself and others, as they reliably deliver delicious food—from a perfectly roasted chicken or grilled steak to expertly prepared fish. The effort pays off in flavorful, satisfying meals that make home cooking truly rewarding. Included here are some helpful tips I've picked up over the past decades.

**Make a vinaigrette.** A go-with-everything vinaigrette is quick and easy to prepare, cheaper than store-bought versions, and better for you. Making it directly in the salad bowl means one fewer dish to clean up: Mix a pinch of granulated sugar (my secret ingredient) with rice vinegar (or white wine vinegar) and a little Dijon mustard, then season with kosher salt and freshly ground pepper. Gradually add extra-virgin olive oil in a slow, steady stream, whisking until the vinaigrette is thickened and emulsified. You can also combine everything in a mason jar and shake to combine; it will keep for about a week in the refrigerator. Feel free to experiment with the quantities, swap fresh lemon juice for the vinegar, or embellish with minced garlic or shallot and/or finely chopped fresh herbs, such as parsley, thyme, or tarragon. It pairs with all types of salads—lettuce, grain, bean, potato, even pasta—and works as a marinade for fish and chicken.

> ▶ **MARTHA COOKS**
>
> I have always been enamored of salads. I remember the very first really great one I ate. It was served as its own course and dressed tableside by an aproned waiter in a small restaurant on the Left Bank in Paris. He took immense pleasure in mixing the vinaigrette in two large spoons over the bowl of just-washed, buttery-soft lettuce leaves.
>
> First, he dissolved coarse sea salt in fragrant wine vinegar in the bowl of one spoon, crushing the crystals with the other spoon. Next, he added olive oil, stirring carefully between every few drops, and sprinkled in a few finely chopped tarragon leaves and freshly ground pepper. He then drizzled the finished dressing over the leaves, which he tossed delicately with the spoons. Finally, he lifted the leaves, one by one, onto a large plate and layered them carefully into a soft mound. I savored that salad and learned my lesson well: Always handle greens with care. As a result, I never grasp a head of Bibb lettuce and tear off its stem or crush the long leaves of romaine before placing them in a bowl. I begin with thoroughly washed and spun-dry greens. (I find that they're a bit crisper if they're chilled afterward, too.) Next up is preparing and using the right amount of a delicious dressing, tossing everything at the very last minute before serving. And last, but most important of all, is to work with the very best ingredients—high-quality oils, tasty vinegars, coarse or flaky sea salts, freshly ground pepper, and farm-fresh vegetables—and to be careful not to overpower the flavors with one too-strong ingredient.

**Make an omelet.** A classic egg dish, an omelet can be served for breakfast, brunch, lunch, even dinner. These steps ensure the fluffiest results: Begin with fresh eggs and remove them from the refrigerator 30 minutes before you begin. Use 3 large eggs per omelet, whisking them with a balloon whisk in a bowl with a pinch of kosher salt and some freshly ground pepper. Heat an 8-inch pan over medium-high for 30 seconds, then coat with a tablespoon of butter. Once the foam subsides, pour the eggs into the center and swirl to coat evenly while running a silicone spatula or a fork in a figure-eight motion until the eggs are just set around the edges, about 30 seconds. The omelet will still be wet in the middle but will continue to cook off heat. Run the spatula around the edge of the omelet to loosen. Tilt the pan toward a serving plate and with the spatula, fold one-third of the omelet over the center. Then roll the omelet onto a plate. Sprinkle with fresh herbs, such as chopped scallions, if desired. Of course, an omelet is a canvas for diverse fillings—grated hard cheese; wilted spinach or other greens; sautéed mushrooms, onions, or other vegetables; and fresh or oven-roasted tomatoes.

**Cook rice and other grains.** For individual grains with a buttery flavor, follow these steps: Rinse the rice well in a fine-mesh sieve until the water runs clear; this removes the surface starches that promote clumping. Use a ratio of 1 cup of water to 1 cup of rice, rather than the usual 2-to-1 ratio. Bring the water to a boil with a pinch of kosher salt and a tablespoon of butter, add the rice, return to a boil, then reduce to a simmer, cover, and cook for 16 minutes. Remove from the heat and let stand another 10 minutes before removing the lid and fluffing with a fork. See the chart on page 36 for how to prepare other whole grains.

**Bread chicken, pork, or fish for frying.** Chicken or pork cutlets, fish fries, and many other favorite dishes rely on having a crisp, golden-brown crust to be delicious. It's as simple as mastering a three-step breading method (see page 39) for success every time.

**Roast a chicken.** Weeknight dinners are where a simple roasted chicken—an iconic comfort food—really shines, though it is equally appropriate for a dinner party. It's even worth roasting a chicken (as described on page 40) on one day and then using the meat in various meals over the next few days—shredded into tacos or quesadillas, sliced into salads or soups, or baked into casseroles. A roasted chicken is an excellent alternative to poached for making creamy chicken salad, too. To turn the bird into a meal-in-one, roast it atop a bed of vegetables, which will soak up the juices in the oven and become flavorful sides. Bonus: The drippings are the foundation of a delicious pan gravy.

**Grill a steak.** Grilling produces a distinct smoky flavor that is not easily replicated by other methods. It also allows for even cooking and temperature control, preventing a tough, overcooked steak. High grill heat initiates the Maillard reaction, a chemical process that browns the steak's surface, creating a flavorful, crispy crust and the signature grill marks. It also cooks the steak quickly, helping the internal marbling melt, which keeps the inside of the steak juicy and tender. See pages 42–45 for additional information.

**Prepare fish.** Many home cooks shy away from cooking fish, thinking it is too challenging. Yet fish lends itself to basic methods (as described on pages 46–47), is a lean source of protein, and cooks relatively quickly—so it really should become part of your weekday routine. A few prerequisites: Always purchase seafood from a trusted source and inspect it for a clean, fresh odor. Fillets should be firm and slightly springy, not flaky or shredded, while a whole fish should have clear, bright eyes, firm scales, and red or pink, unblemished gills. Buy fish as close to the cooking time as possible and store it in the coldest part of your refrigerator until ready to cook.

# Martha's Secret to Cooking Whole Grains

**The chart below is meant as a guide for cooking 1 cup of grains by the absorption method: Bring water (or stock), grains, and a pinch of kosher salt to a boil, reduce to a simmer, cover tightly, and cook until the grains are tender and have absorbed all the liquid; then let stand for an additional 10 minutes off the heat (still covered) before fluffing with a fork. The amount of liquid and cooking times vary depending on the type of grain as well as your preference for chewy versus tender texture (hence the ranges provided). Note that presoaking the grains will also help make them tender. For deeper flavor, toast the grains in the pan with a little oil or butter before adding the water, shaking the pan until they have a nutty aroma.**

| Whole Grain | Amount of Water | Cooking Time |
|---|---|---|
| **▶ AMARANTH** <br> This small herb seed has a slightly peppery taste and is actually not a grain. (It's one of three pseudograins that are treated like a grain because of their nutritional and culinary profiles.) Use it to add protein, fiber, and a nutty flavor to a variety of dishes, including breakfast porridge, granola, and muffins, or as a gluten-free alternative to grains in some recipes. Amaranth can even be popped like popcorn or cooked like rice or quinoa. | 2 cups | 20 minutes |
| **▶ BARLEY** <br> With its trademark chewy, toothsome texture and mild, nutty flavor, barley is perfect for adding to soups, stews, and salads, as well as for soaking up the flavors of other ingredients in a dish. When buying barley, look for hulled or hull-less varieties over pearl. | 3 cups | 35 to 40 minutes |
| **▶ BROWN RICE** <br> Since it still contains the bran and germ, brown rice has more fiber and essential minerals than white rice. It also has a more pronounced (nutty) taste and is both denser and less tender than its milled counterpart, in addition to being less starchy—no rinsing required. The shorter the grain, the more starchy it will be. | 2 cups | 35 to 45 minutes |
| **▶ BUCKWHEAT** <br> Despite its name, buckwheat is another pseudograin that is botanically a seed; it is harvested from a flowering plant related to rhubarb. Today, it's on-trend as a gluten-free alternative to regular flour or for adding a robust, earthy flavor (and distinctive color) to pancakes and baked goods. It is also prized as a complete plant-based source of protein. But it has a rich history in Japan and Korea, where it appears in soba and other traditional noodles, and in Eastern Europe, where the groats are used in stuffed vegetables or to make a type of porridge called kasha. Whole buckwheat groats can be found raw or toasted. | 2 cups | 15 minutes |
| **▶ BULGUR** <br> Best known as a key ingredient in tabbouleh and other Middle Eastern dishes, bulgur is a type of cracked wheat that is parboiled during its production, so it cooks relatively quickly while retaining the fiber and nutrition of a whole grain. Enjoy it as a side dish for chicken, incorporated into a vegetable burger, soup, or stuffing, or as a hot breakfast cereal, packed with nutrients and fiber. | 2 cups | 20 minutes |

| Whole Grain | Amount of Water | Cooking Time |
|---|---|---|
| ▶ **FARRO**<br>This high-fiber, high-protein, flavorful ancient wheat grain is popular in Mediterranean cuisine and as a substitute for rice (it makes a delicious risotto) or pasta. The Italian word "farro" refers to three different grains—einkorn, emmer, and spelt—though emmer is the most common type found today. It holds up well in soups, salads, and pilafs. Look for semi-pearled farro, which retains more of its bran and germ than that labeled as pearled. | 3 cups | 30 to 35 minutes |
| ▶ **KAMUT**<br>Kamut (aka Khorasan) wheat is another ancient grain, featuring large kernels, a firm texture, and a rich, buttery taste. It is an excellent source of protein and, though not suitable for anyone with celiac disease, can often be tolerated by those who are gluten sensitive. Whole kamut berries can be used in place of wheat berries or rice in pilafs, casseroles, and both warm and cold salads. Like many other grains, it makes a delicious hot breakfast porridge. | 3 cups | 45 to 50 minutes |
| ▶ **MILLET**<br>Millet (along with teff and sorghum) is one of the "nutri-cereals," so named because of their high nutrient content. Because it is prone to being sticky, it is important to wash it well before using; toasting it with or without a little oil will also help. Use it in both sweet and savory recipes, including breakfast bowls, muesli, vegetable burgers, pilafs, and grain salads. | 2 cups | 30 to 35 minutes |
| ▶ **OATS**<br>Unlike the more familiar old-fashioned rolled oats, whole (hulled) oat groats remain chewy and take longer to cook. You can use them as you would wheat berries—in grain bowls or salads, pilafs, soups, stews, and hot cereal. Toast them to bring out their nuttiness. | 1 cup | 60 minutes |
| ▶ **QUINOA**<br>The third pseudograin in the bunch, quinoa (which hails from South America) is a popular gluten-free, protein-rich base for hot cereals, grain salads, vegetable burgers, pilafs, and so much more. Quinoa can also be added to breads, cookies, muffins, and other baked goods. The most commonly available varieties in the US are red, brown, black, and ivory. You can also buy tricolor blends. They are all interchangeable in recipes; choose your color preference. Be sure to rinse quinoa to remove the bitter coating. | 2 cups | 15 minutes |
| ▶ **SPELT**<br>An heirloom variety of wheat popular in parts of Europe, spelt is prized for its subtle sweetness and high fiber. While it is not suitable for anyone with celiac disease, spelt's water-soluble gluten may be easier to digest for those with mild wheat sensitivities. In flour form, it is widely used in bread baking. | 3 cups | 45 minutes |
| ▶ **WHEAT BERRIES**<br>As the complete, unprocessed wheat grain, wheat berries contain the nutritious bran, germ, and endosperm. One cup of the berries delivers over 15 grams of protein and a significant amount of fiber and iron. You can use wheat berries in salads and soups, and as a stuffing for peppers or other vegetables. Or grind the whole berries to make whole wheat flour. | 2½ to 3 cups | 30 to 40 minutes |

# Three-Step Breading How-To

The traditional breading method involves coating food sequentially in flour (to create a dry surface), eggs (the "glue"), and breadcrumbs (for crunch) to make an extra-crispy, well-adhered crust. When using this on fish, opt for mild, lean but firm, flaky white types, including catfish, cod, flounder, haddock, perch, and tilapia; meatier fish such as grouper, halibut, and red snapper are other options.

## 1
Dredge the food in seasoned all-purpose flour to coat it evenly. Shake off any excess flour.

## 2
Dip the food into a lightly beaten egg or egg wash, allowing any excess to drip off.

## 3
Dredge the egg-coated food in the breadcrumbs, turning it to coat both sides. Press the crumbs gently and firmly to ensure they adhere well. For the crispiest result, use panko breadcrumbs.

## Secrets to Success

▸ **SET UP A BREADING STATION**
Arrange three shallow dishes side by side for an efficient assembly line. Keep one hand "dry" for the flour and breadcrumbs and the other "wet" for the egg to avoid a clumpy mess.

▸ **SEASON EVERY LAYER**
For the best flavor, season the food itself as well as each of the three breading components with kosher salt and freshly ground pepper. You can also add dried herbs, grated Parmesan cheese, or ground spices to the flour or breadcrumbs for extra flavor.

▸ **CHILL BEFORE COOKING**
After breading, put the food in the refrigerator for about 15 minutes to help the coating set and adhere firmly, so it won't fall off during cooking. You can even freeze the cutlets at this point, which is a great way to prep for busy nights: Flash freeze them in a single layer on a parchment-lined baking sheet until firm, then transfer them to an airtight freezer bag or container for longer storage (up to 3 months). The breaded cutlets don't even need to be thawed before cooking; they can go straight from the freezer to the pan.

▸ **MAINTAIN OIL HEAT**
If pan-frying, use an oil with a high smoke point, such as grapeseed, avocado, canola, or peanut, and heat it to between 350°F and 375°F. Cook the coated food in batches to avoid overcrowding the pan and lowering the oil temperature. Remove any browned crumbs from the oil with a slotted spoon between batches to prevent the chicken from burning. Also, allow the oil to return to 350°F to 375°F before adding the next batch.

# Roasted Chicken 101

It's often been said that the ultimate test of a chef (or a home cook) is their ability to make a perfect roasted chicken—because simplicity is not always easy. There are many ways to make a delicious chicken and even more ways to make it not quite as good as it could be. Decades of advice are distilled here into a go-to method that can be easily adapted to suit the season or occasion.

## Secrets to Success

**▶ BUY**

When possible, purchase a humanely raised whole organic chicken (3 to 4 pounds) from a reliable source. Fresh will always taste better than frozen.

**▶ PREP**

Rinsing raw chicken increases the risk of foodborne illnesses, and the cooking process will kill any surface bacteria. Do pat the exterior with paper towels—the drier the skin, the crispier it will get. Remove the giblets from the cavity and reserve. Season the cavity with salt and pepper, then tuck in a halved lemon, fresh thyme sprigs, and whole peeled garlic cloves.

**▶ TRUSS**

Trussing ensures that the chicken will remain in a tidy bundle and the meat will cook evenly. Tuck the wing tips under to keep them from burning; also tuck the neck flap under. Then tie butcher's twine around the bird, wrapping it just above the neck opening and under and over each drumstick, pulling those tight and securing the twine with a knot.

**▶ DRY BRINE**

Seasoning the chicken generously with salt (and desired spices) and leaving it in the refrigerator overnight ensures that each bite is perfectly flavored. It also dries out the skin for the crispiest results. (You can skip this step, being sure to season with lots of salt and pepper before roasting.)

**▶ BRING TO ROOM TEMPERATURE**

Remove the chicken from the refrigerator 1 hour before cooking. When a cold bird is placed in a hot oven, the outside will cook more quickly than the inside, resulting in either dry or undercooked parts.

**▶ PREP THE PAN**

Place the chicken in a heavy-bottomed roasting pan fitted with a rack, allowing the fat to drip off and air to circulate around the bird. Or rest the bird on slices of onion, carrots, or potatoes, which can be served alongside.

**▶ COOK UNTIL DONE**

Roast in a preheated 450°F oven, positioning the drumsticks near the rear of the oven (the hottest part). Baste with softened butter or drizzle with olive oil. It's ready when a meat thermometer inserted into the thickest part of a thigh registers 165°F, which can take approximately 50 minutes. The skin should also be nicely browned.

**▶ LET IT REST**

Allowing the bird to rest will prevent the juices from escaping when sliced, causing the meat to be dry. You can remove the trussing during this time.

**▶ MAKE THE PAN GRAVY**

Remove the rack (or the vegetables) from the roasting pan, and pour off all but a little of the rendered fat, leaving the browned bits behind. Place the pan over two burners set to high heat. Deglaze it with about ½ cup white wine, stirring with a flat-edge wooden spoon to scrape the caramelized juices, and boil until reduced. Stir in one or two pats of butter to enrich the sauce. Strain through a fine-mesh sieve, season to taste, and serve with the chicken.

# How to Grill Great Steaks

Cooking meat on a smoking-hot grill requires careful preparation and monitoring to achieve steakhouse results every time. Even home grill masters will appreciate having the following steps and recommended cooking times for choice cuts as a handy guide.

## Secrets to Success

▸ **PREPARE THE GRILL**

**Gas:** Heat on medium-high with the top closed for 15 minutes. Then turn off one burner, so you can finish cooking thicker pieces over indirect heat or move steaks to avoid flare-ups.

**Charcoal:** Light a pile of coals (a chimney works best). When they're uniformly gray with red embers, spread them over three-fourths of the bottom rack, creating direct and indirect zones (as described for the gas grill above). Replace the top rack; heat, covered, for about 10 minutes.

▸ **TEST THE TEMPERATURE**

Hold your hand about 3 inches from the grates; when you can keep it there for 5 to 7 seconds, the grill has reached medium heat; for 3 to 4 seconds (no longer), the grill has reached high heat.

▸ **PREP THE MEAT**

Remove the meat from the refrigerator at least 30 minutes beforehand to ensure even cooking. About 15 minutes before you start, brush both sides of the meat with vegetable oil, and season generously with kosher salt and freshly ground pepper. Scrape the grill grates clean with a wire brush while they're hot, then oil them just before cooking.

▸ **POSITION THE MEAT**

Cook steaks that are 1½ inches thick or less uncovered over direct medium-high heat. For anything thicker (say, large porterhouses and rib eyes), start over direct heat; after the times noted in the chart on page 44, transfer to indirect heat, cover, and finish cooking to the temperatures listed, so they can cook through without burning. For defined grill marks, wait to move or flip the meat until you see a nice char on the first side.

▸ **TEST FOR DONENESS**

Insert an instant-read thermometer into the thickest part of the steaks from the side (begin at the low end of the time range, subtracting a minute or so if you prefer rare meat). Recommended temperatures: 120°F for rare, 125°F to 130°F for medium-rare, 135°F to 140°F for medium, 145°F to 155°F for medium-well, and above 155°F for well-done.

▸ **LET IT REST**

Once you remove the steak from the grill, let it sit for 10 minutes, tented with foil. The residual heat will finish the cooking, and the juices will have time to redistribute throughout for optimal flavor. For the best texture, slice the meat against the grain.

▸ **SERVE**

Steak is perfectly fine on its own, sliced and served with your preferred sides. But for a pretty presentation, top a sliced flank steak with peppery greens, like arugula, squeeze lemon quarters over the greens, and season with kosher salt and freshly ground pepper. A thicker cut (such as the rib eye on page 45) can be spread with jalapeño butter and flaky sea salt, and served with Upland Cress and sliced white onion alongside.

# Grilling Primer

**Everyone should know how to prepare a great steak—it's simple yet transformative, blending basic cooking fundamentals with impressive results. The following chart provides general recommendations for cooking it to medium-rare; but if you prefer it more or less done, simply see the internal temperature ranges below.**

| Choice Cut | Cooking Time |
|---|---|
| **▶ RIB EYE** <br> A classic for a reason, this splurge-worthy piece is delectable, whether boneless or bone-in. It's sliced from the rib for well-marbled, flavor-rich bites. | **6 to 8 minutes per side for a 1½-inch-thick boneless steak, slightly longer for bone-in** |
| **▶ PORTERHOUSE** <br> This piece is two steaks in one: The large side is the New York strip, and the smaller side is the mild-tasting tenderloin. Two and a half pounds will serve four. Cut slices off the bone so everyone can have a piece of both. | **6 to 8 minutes per side for a 1½-inch-thick steak** |
| **▶ SKIRT** <br> Taken from just under the ribs, this cut is long and flat. It has fat content throughout, which lends extra juiciness and makes it nearly impossible to dry out. | **2 minutes per side for thinner pieces; 3 to 5 minutes for thicker ones** |
| **▶ TOP SIRLOIN** <br> Cut from the loin between the ribs and the round, this boneless piece is naturally lean but still packed with flavor. Standard sirloin tends to be tougher. | **4 to 6 minutes per side for a 1-inch-thick steak** |
| **▶ NEW YORK STRIP** <br> Strip steak makes a bold statement for a special occasion, offering rich, intense flavor. It's cut from the short loin and has a firm texture, so be careful not to overcook it. | **4 to 6 minutes per side for a 1- to 1¼-inch-thick boneless steak** |
| **▶ FLANK** <br> This boneless steak comes from the muscle just below the loin. Again, take care not to overcook it—you'll be rewarded with deep flavor and tender bites. | **4 to 6 minutes per side for a 1- to 1¼-inch-thick steak** |

## Recommended Temperatures

| Rare: <br> **120°F** | Medium-rare: <br> **125°F to 130°F** | Medium: <br> **135°F to 140°F** | Medium-well: <br> **145°F to 155°F** | Well-done: <br> **above 155°F** |
|---|---|---|---|---|

# Fish Primer

The following methods are classic and widely employed for all kinds of proteins and produce. Here, they are demystified so you know which one works best for different types of fish—and for you.

## ▶ SAUTÉING

**Best for:** A flaky, mild-tasting fish, such as lemon sole or flounder, works best. Pacific-caught varieties are the most sustainable. Tilapia works well, too.

**How-to:** Season the fish with kosher salt and freshly ground pepper, dust with Wondra flour (to encourage a delicate crust to form), and cook rapidly in a pan with a little fat over relatively high heat. Butter will create more browning than oil. Lemon slices and herbs can be added after flipping the fish halfway through.

**Pros:** Sautéing showcases the fish's delicate texture and yields tender, lightly browned food in just 10 minutes. You can also create a quick sauce using the pan drippings.

**Tips:** Always sauté fish just before serving. Serve with steamed new potatoes and sautéed spinach.

## ▶ SLOW-ROASTING

**Best for:** This method is ideal for thick fillets of a fatty fish, such as wild salmon. Alaskan sockeye has a rich flavor; king is pricier and fattier. If you like, try Tasmanian ocean trout as an alternative.

**How-to:** Generously season the fillets with kosher salt and freshly ground pepper, place in a lightly greased baking dish, and oven-roast at a very low temperature (250°F) until they're opaque on the outside and medium-rare in the center, about 25 minutes. The key is to avoid overcooking, so be sure to monitor the cooking time and test for doneness.

**Pros:** Low-and-slow cooking produces fish with a perfect melt-in-your-mouth texture.

**Tips:** Add halved cherry tomatoes and basil to the baking dish before roasting. Serve with tabbouleh and toasted pita.

### ▶ POACHING

**Best for:** Whole fish, such as wild salmon or pink-fleshed arctic char, is as easy to poach as a fillet. Poaching is also great for cooking leaner fish, such as flounder, sole, cod, and tilapia, that are prone to drying out.

**How-to:** To poach, submerge the fish in a gently simmering liquid such as court bouillon, other stocks, or water flavored with aromatics, including whole peppercorns or other spices, sliced citrus, herbs, and vegetables. Keep the liquid almost at a simmer (between 160°F and 185°F)—you shouldn't see any bubbles. You may want to tie fillets in cheesecloth to prevent breakage.

**Pros:** This method yields tender, juicy results, with subtle flavor from the poaching liquid.

**Tips:** Whisk some of the poaching liquid with equal parts olive oil for drizzling over the fish. For a refreshing lunch, serve the poached fish chilled on a bed of fresh or wilted baby greens (arugula, spinach, or kale) and topped with a creamy horseradish sauce. Serve it warm with puréed vegetables on the side for a heartier dinner.

### ▶ STEAMING

**Best for:** Thick and meaty halibut steaks are delicious when steamed. Also try salmon steaks or Pacific cod.

**How-to:** This method works equally well with a stackable bamboo steamer basket or a collapsible metal basket. Bring about 2 inches of water to a boil in a pot (or a wok if using a bamboo basket). Season the fish with salt and pepper, then place it in the basket, leaving room for the steam to circulate and ensure even, rapid cooking. Cover and steam over simmering water until opaque throughout, 6 to 10 minutes.

**Pros:** Steaming in a closed vessel surrounds the fish with water vapor to produce clean, clear flavors. This indirect, moist heat cooks food gently, quickly, and without much added fat and with minimal loss of nutrients.

**Tips:** Line the steamer basket with cabbage, banana leaves, or fresh herbs to infuse the fish. Serve with a squeeze of lime and asparagus cooked in the second layer of the bamboo steamer (or in a separate pot). Try different stocks in place of the simmering water.

### ▶ PARCHMENT-BAKING

**Best for:** Top choices include striped bass and other mild, firm-fleshed fish (such as cod, halibut, or wild salmon); fine-textured tilapia is another lovely alternative.

**How-to:** Cooking en papillote (the French term) involves wrapping the fillet in a single-serving parchment packet: Place the fillet off-center on a sheet of parchment, then fold it over and crimp the edges, from end to end, to seal tightly, forming a half-moon shape. Place on a baking sheet and bake at 350°F until the package is puffy and the paper has browned, about 12 minutes.

**Pros:** As with traditional steaming methods, parchment-baking locks in the moisture so the fish doesn't dry out (a common complaint). Consider adding vegetables, like thinly sliced asparagus and leeks, to the package. Finally, snipping the parcel open at the table with kitchen scissors makes for an impressive presentation.

**Tips:** Mix soy sauce with a pinch of sugar and drizzle it over the fish, then sprinkle it with julienned fresh ginger. Serve with brown or white rice and steamed bok choy.

# 6

# ESTABLISH GOOD KITCHEN HABITS

The lessons here are largely derived from what professional chefs are taught so they can deliver excellent results in a high-paced environment. But they apply just as much to a home kitchen, where efficiency, food safety, and enjoyment are important factors.

**Read a recipe all the way through.** Though you may be eager to get cooking—or on a tight schedule—it's important to take the time to carefully read a recipe from start to finish before you begin. First, this allows you to plan your shopping ahead of time, avoiding any unpleasant surprises—like discovering you are out of brown sugar or don't have the right-size pan when you are halfway through the steps. Second, it allows you to properly plan out your timeline: You certainly don't want to find out that you need to marinate the chicken overnight for that day's dinner.

**Practice mise en place.** Prepare all the ingredients for a recipe at the start, including measuring and chopping; this is known as mise en place. The process of gathering and measuring forces you to slow down and consider the elements of the recipe. It also keeps you organized as you follow the steps, so you'll be much less likely to leave an ingredient out—or end up burning something while searching for the next item. Finally, having all your ingredients at the ready means they will be at the appropriate temperature, such as eggs that need to be at room temperature or butter that needs to be well-chilled, for baking.

**Know how to measure ingredients.** Improvising is fine when roasting or grilling, but baking requires more precision. It is particularly essential when measuring flour for baking, as too much (the usual error) will result in overly dry, heavy baked goods.

> ▸ **MARTHA COOKS**
> Employ the "fluff, spoon, and level" method to measure flour: Use a fork or a balloon whisk to fluff the flour in its container; spoon the flour into the appropriate-size dry measure cup, filling it generously; last, run the back of a knife across the top of the cup to level it, sweeping the excess flour back into the container. Do not shake or tap the cup on the counter.

**Clean as you go.** Keep your workspace and tools clean as you work. Move emptied dishes, as well as dirty utensils and pans, to the sink after use, and clean them while multitasking (such as while the soup is simmering). Wipe up spills right away. Doing this reduces the risk of cross-contamination, accidents, and recipe mistakes. It also makes cleaning up at the end more manageable.

**Have a scrap bowl nearby for composting.** This makes it so you can quickly sweep away all the trimmings when prepping produce and other ingredients. Knowing what can and cannot be composted is also essential: Fruits and vegetables, herbs, eggshells, coffee grounds and used filters, loose tea and tea bags (without staples), and even leftovers like cooked pasta, rice, and other grains are all considered "green" materials. Do not compost meat, poultry, fish (including the bones), dairy products, cooking fats and oils, or any greasy foods. (See page 222 for more on home composting.)

**Monitor your oven temperature.** Not all ovens are accurate in terms of the actual heat inside matching the dial setting, which increases the risk of under- or overcooking roasts and baked goods. The solution? Buy an inexpensive oven thermometer that stays inside your oven for accurate preheating and monitoring during cooking. Place it in the center of the oven, where you can read it through the oven window to avoid opening the door.

**Trust your senses.** Consider cooking times as guidelines rather than strict rules. Lots of variables can impact when a dish is done. Most recipes offer visual or other sensory indicators, relying on thermometers when accuracy is important, such as when cooking poultry or pork. Tasting (and seasoning) certain items as you go is another way to ensure a successful outcome.

**Rely on the freezer.** Devote one day a week or month to making big batches of cooked grains, beans, stocks, tomato sauces, ragùs, and other building blocks to store in the freezer. Many soups, stews, chilis, casseroles, and baked pastas also freeze well, as do breaded cutlets (see page 39), burritos, and a host of baked goods, including muffins, scones, biscuits, and quick breads.

# On-the-Spot Substitutions

**Flag this handy chart for the next time you're ready to cook, only to realize you are missing a crucial component—and it's too late (or inconvenient) to dash to the store. Here are clever swaps for common ingredients; use an equal amount called for in the recipe unless otherwise noted.**

| Missing Item | What It Brings | Smart Swap |
|---|---|---|
| ▸ **KOSHER SALT** | Salt amplifies the flavor of both savory and sweet preparations when added during cooking. | ½ teaspoon table or fine sea salt for every 1 teaspoon kosher (Diamond Crystal). |
| ▸ **DIJON MUSTARD** | The condiment delivers spice, tang, and vinegary punch. It also thickens pan sauces and enriches and emulsifies vinaigrettes and other salad dressings. | Grainy or spicy brown mustard, or yellow mustard mixed with a tiny dollop of prepared horseradish. |
| ▸ **TOMATO PASTE** | It's the secret to adding intensity to any tomato-based sauce. You can also fry a spoonful with aromatics for a hint of sweetness and acidity when cooking a pot roast or stew. | Ketchup; or simmer down double the amount of canned tomato sauce or purée. |
| ▸ **FISH SAUCE** | This South Asian staple offers bright, briny notes and deep umami flavor to sauces, soups, stews, stir-fries, and so much more. A little goes a very, very long way. | Equal parts soy sauce and rice vinegar, mixed with 1 minced anchovy. |
| ▸ **CAPERS** | These pickled delicacies deliver salty, briny, zingy flavor when sprinkled on salads, added to sauces, or tossed with roasting vegetables halfway through the cook time. | Chopped cornichons or mild green olives. |
| ▸ **SHALLOTS** | A member of the allium family, shallots lend subtle sweetness and a slight bite to vinaigrettes, salad dressings, and braised dishes—think onion meets garlic. | Red or white onions or leeks, plus a pinch of minced garlic. |
| ▸ **FRESH TENDER HERBS** (parsley, mint, basil, dill, cilantro, tarragon) | They add lively, aromatic notes to a wide range of dishes and drinks, typically as a last-minute addition or garnish. | The same amount of another tender herb. |
| ▸ **FRESH HARDY HERBS** (thyme, oregano, rosemary, marjoram) | These herbs lend sweet and woodsy tastes to a pan of roasted chicken or vegetables, as well as depth of flavor when sautéed with mirepoix for a soup or stew. | The same amount of another hardy herb, or half the amount of dried. |

# 7

# DEVELOP A RECIPE REPERTOIRE

Today's busy schedules make it challenging to prepare meals for yourself or your family, so having a roster of trusted recipes can be your ally. You won't have to spend time searching for what to make for dinner. Plus, you will already be familiar with the ingredients and process, making weekday cooking more manageable.

**Make a list of trusted recipes.** Begin by collecting recipes you love and know turn out great every time. Be sure to cover the different seasons: produce-heavy salads and pasta dishes, refreshing soups and risottos or other grain-centric meals, and sautéed or grilled proteins for spring and summer; heartier stews, roasts, and baked pastas for fall and winter.

**Try some different cooking techniques.** Add some recipes to your list that require different or more advanced cooking techniques. For example, once you master the methods for cooking fish described on page 46, you can find other applications—such as pan-fried pork chops, poached or steamed chicken breasts, or slow-roasted tofu (possibly the best way to cook it). And if you love oven-roasted carrots, employ the same process for turnips, parsnips, rutabaga, celeriac, beets, and other root vegetables.

**Add variations of your mainstays.** This is a wonderful way to create new dishes and grow your collection organically. One simple strategy is to make seasonal swaps, so your gnocchi with tomatoes and basil in the summer shifts to butternut squash and sage in the fall. Or if your default side dish is brown rice, try another whole grain like spelt or bulgur—and use farro in place of Arborio rice for a risotto. (See the chart on page 36 for other whole grains.) Another easy substitution is to find rare or heirloom varieties of the produce you like most, whether it's Japanese purple sweet potatoes, Golden Bantam corn, or Dragon Tongue green beans. This approach is another excellent reason to shop farmers' markets or to grow your own (and from seed).

**Include make-ahead recipes.** Consider recipes that can be prepared entirely or partially ahead of time and then simply reheated on a busy weeknight. Or double recipes that keep well to serve as dinner one night and lunch the next day. This category is vast and ranges from soups, stews, and braises that tend to improve over time to grain bowls (tossing everything together before serving), cold pasta or noodle dishes, roasted chicken (the perfect eat-now-use-the-rest-later dish), pot roast (ditto), and more.

**Incorporate variety.** Subscribing to the tips above will automatically ensure you have different flavor profiles, protein sources, colorful produce, and cooking methods. However, you should still be intentional about rotating among poultry, fish, and meat-free options to avoid repetition. The same applies to switching up the seasonings—and occasionally experimenting with special ingredients—like black truffles in angel-hair pasta (at right)—to keep meals (and preparing them) more interesting.

# 8

# BOLSTER YOUR BAKING SKILLS

If you love baking as much as I do, you'll appreciate the importance of knowing the tools, techniques, ingredients, and tricks to producing absolutely delicious sweets to enjoy and share with your family and friends all year long.

**Buy the necessary tools.** Most home cooks own assorted cake pans and muffin tins, but it's worth picking up extras that experienced bakers rely on to take your baking skills to the next level. These include:

▶ measuring cups, for both dry and wet ingredients;

▶ a bench scraper, for moving around ingredients and cleaning flour off your counter;

▶ pastry brushes, for buttering pans and applying egg washes and glazes;

▶ a rolling pin—preferably a slightly tapered wood model;

▶ an offset serrated knife with a jagged edge, for chopping chocolate and nuts, and a raised handle to protect your fingers;

▶ parchment paper, for lining pans to prevent items from sticking and make cleanup easier.

**Stock up on staples.** You never know when the urge to bake will strike, so here's what to keep on hand. Remember: Quality is key.

▶ Flour: Unbleached all-purpose flour is the default for baking; gluten-free products such as Cup4Cup or Measure for Measure by King Arthur let you replace it in equal amounts. Whole wheat flours, including spelt, lend flavor and texture; replace half of all-purpose flour with one of these flours for a more wholesome product.

▶ Sugar: Granulated sugar and brown sugar give baked goods their sweetness; turbinado sugar and coconut sugar are popular alternatives. Confectioners' sugar is most frequently dusted on finished items or used to make royal icing.

▶ Dutch-process cocoa powder renders a darker color and milder flavor than regular (non-alkalized) cocoa.

▶ Baking powder and baking soda are essential leavening agents that allow baked goods to rise.

▶ Vanilla extract adds flavor; vanilla beans provide a more pronounced result.

**Start from scratch.** Besides their superior taste and freshness, homemade baked goods let you control the quality of the ingredients, so you know exactly what you are eating. You can also swap in healthier flours and other ingredients for a more wholesome product. And if you find that most baked goods turn out too sweet for your palate, you can reduce the sugar up to 25 percent without jeopardizing the integrity of the recipe (any more, and the structure, moisture, and browning levels could be affected). Those with food allergies or sensitivities will appreciate how many of their favorite baked goods can be modified by creating them in their own kitchen. Factor in that scratch-baked goods cost a lot less than anything from a bakery or a store, too. See page 62 for a tutorial on piecrust—easily the most intimidating task for home bakers.

**Focus on universal favorites.** When it comes to building a dessert repertoire, a good place to start is with surefire crowd-pleasers, even if the "crowd" consists of yourself and your family or friends. The six best-loved treats—chocolate chip cookies, brownies, pound cake, cheesecake, rhubarb-strawberry pie, and chocolate frosted layer cake—will cover all your everyday and special occasion needs, and then some. See pages 66–77 for easy ways to elevate and enjoy your go-to recipes.

# Baking Substitutions

**Memorize (or keep a record of) common baking substitutions, including the instructions for brown sugar and buttermilk:**

| Missing Item | What It Brings | Smart Swap |
|---|---|---|
| ▶ **VANILLA** | Whether using freshly scraped seeds or a quality bottled extract, vanilla is a versatile ingredient that makes baked goods taste more complete (much like salt), creating a smoother, more aromatic, and nuanced final product. | Use 1 teaspoon vanilla extract to replace the seeds from half a pod. An equal amount of bourbon, maple syrup, or honey can be used in place of extract. |
| ▶ **BROWN SUGAR** | It imparts moisture and a chewy texture in baked goods, along with a richer, deeper flavor than white, which is also prized in barbecue and other sauces. | 1 cup granulated sugar plus 2 tablespoons molasses equals 1 cup brown sugar (light or dark). |
| ▶ **BAKING POWDER/SODA** | These chemical leaveners make baked goods rise and become light and fluffy, but they work differently: Baking soda needs an acid (like buttermilk) to activate for lift, and also promotes browning and spreading; baking powder simply requires liquid and then heat to create a double-acting rise. | Use ½ teaspoon cream of tartar combined with ¼ teaspoon baking soda for every 1 teaspoon baking powder, or 1 teaspoon baking powder for every ¼ teaspoon baking soda (with tangier outcomes). |
| ▶ **CAKE FLOUR** | A finely milled flour made from soft wheat, cake flour has a low protein content for less gluten development, resulting in baked goods (notably angel food and chiffon cakes) that are exceptionally tender, light, and fluffy with a fine, even crumb. | All-purpose flour can be used instead of cake flour cup for cup, replacing 2 tablespoons AP with 2 tablespoons cornstarch. |
| ▶ **SELF-RISING FLOUR** | The primary benefit is convenience because it provides built-in leavening, so you don't need to add extra rising agents to the recipe. | To substitute 1 cup self-rising flour, use 1 cup all-purpose flour plus 1½ teaspoons baking powder and ¼ teaspoon kosher salt. |
| ▶ **BUTTERMILK** | It produces tender baked goods (especially biscuits and scones) and meats (when used as a marinade), plus it's the secret to tangy coleslaw, mashed potatoes, and certain salad dressings (like ranch). | For 1 cup buttermilk, mix 1 cup milk or yogurt with 1 tablespoon white vinegar or lemon juice and let it sit for 20 minutes before using. |

# Pâte Brisée Tutorial

With a few simple steps and some trial and error, anyone can learn to mix, roll (or press), and bake an all-butter dough. The following tips and techniques will help ensure the best possible pies, tarts, galettes, and other desserts. Practice also helps—I've been making my pâte brisée recipe for more than 40 years!

**Makes: Enough for one 9-inch double-crust pie, two galettes, or one 10½-by-15¼-inch single-crust slab pie**

**2½** cups unbleached all-purpose flour

**1** tablespoon sugar

**1½** teaspoons kosher salt (Diamond Crystal)

**2** sticks (1 cup) cold unsalted butter, cut into pieces

**¼ to ½** cup ice-cold water

**1.** Pulse flour, sugar, and salt in a food processor until combined. Add butter and pulse until mixture resembles coarse meal, with a few pea-size pieces remaining. Drizzle in ¼ cup ice-cold water and pulse until mixture holds together when pinched. If it doesn't, drizzle up to ¼ cup more water, as needed, 1 tablespoon at a time; pulse. (Do not overprocess; it should look like moist gravel, not a solid mass.)

**2.** For a 9-inch pie or galette, shape dough into two disks, and wrap each in plastic. For a slab pie, shape dough into a rectangle and wrap in plastic. Refrigerate until firm, at least 1 hour and up to 1 day, or freeze up to 3 months; thaw in refrigerator overnight before using.

The finished dough should be mottled with large pieces of butter. The best way to transfer the rolled-out dough to a pie plate is by rolling it over the pin and unfurling it onto the plate.

▶ **PREP**

Start with cold ingredients: Chill all the ingredients—even the dry ones—for 30 minutes. Then cut the butter into cubes before adding to the food processor.

▶ **MIX**

Add the butter and pulse until the mixture resembles coarse meal with some pea-size pieces. Drizzle in the ice-cold water and pulse a few times to test the dough.

▶ **TEST**

The dough should remain crumbly but come together when squeezed. Don't pulse it so long that it forms a ball. If it does, it's overworked.

▶ **TURN OUT**

When you empty the mixture from the food processor onto the plastic wrap, some pieces will be tiny, others will be in clumps. This is exactly what you want. You're on your way to a light, flaky crust.

▶ **PRESS**

Bring the edges of the plastic wrap together to form a round mass, and press on top of the wrap to form a disk. You're simultaneously gathering the crumbs into a cohesive dough and shaping it.

▶ **ROLL**

Roll the dough into rounds that are about ½ inch thick and 8 inches in diameter—as opposed to the standard hockey-puck size—which will chill more quickly and soften more uniformly when removed from the refrigerator.

# Alternative Crusts

If preparing traditional pâte brisée is keeping you from baking pies, know that a few easier options are classics in their own right.

▶ **COOKIE-CRUMB CRUST**

The easiest of all, this is the same familiar crust that you've likely been making for your cheesecakes, only you can substitute crushed gingersnaps, or practically any other cookie for the usual graham crackers (or stick with those). You can even go in a slightly less-sweet direction by using crushed pretzels for a welcome salty kick. The trick to getting the buttery crumb mixture evenly in the pie dish is to press on it with the bottom of a dry measuring spoon, which can reach into the corners.

▶ **SHORTBREAD CRUST**

A tender, sweet shortbread dough is almost as easy. Because the dough isn't rolled out, you don't need a rolling pin—just a mixing bowl and a spoon. Press the buttery, still-crumbly dough evenly into a pie dish, then bake the dough briefly before adding the filling—ideally a satiny pumpkin custard one. The finished crust is crisp and cookie-like.

▶ **CREAM CHEESE CRUST**

A combination of butter and cream cheese produces a forgiving piecrust that's supple and a joy to roll out. (You can simply replace half the butter with cream cheese in most standard pie dough recipes.) The cream cheese also gives the crust a lovely tang that pairs well with rich pecan-pie fillings—plain or enhanced with butterscotch, bourbon, or chocolate. Give it a simple fluted edge for a traditional finishing touch.

# ▶ CLASSIC DESSERT CANON

## Chocolate Chip Cookies

*This chocolate chip cookie is crisp around the edges but still chewy in the center, for the best of both worlds in one delicious package. The following tips will help you achieve that optimal texture as well as inimitable flavor.*

**Creaming:** This step sets up the dough for success and requires butter that is softened but still cool to the touch; it's ready when your fingertip leaves a dent without sinking in deeply. Note: Use this same test for the pound cake—or any recipe that calls for softened or room temperature butter.

**Sweetness:** Mixing different kinds of sugar gives dimension, since granulated is neutral and brown sugar lends caramel notes. Brown sugar also imparts more moisture.

**Gooeyness:** Two forms of chocolate are better than one. Chips hold their shape while chopped shards melt into ribbons.

**Chilling:** "Aging" the dough in the refrigerator for an hour or overnight before baking can promote a deeper flavor, more uniform golden color, and a slightly gooier texture. It also allows you to mix the dough ahead of time for efficiency's sake.

**Scooping:** When it's time to bake, use a 2-ounce (¼-cup) ice-cream scoop for the optimal ratio of sturdy edge to chewy center. For next-level cookies, top each dough portion with a few large, flat pieces of chopped chocolate.

**Spreading:** Twice during baking (about one-third and two-thirds of the way through), remove the cookie sheet and bang it on the stove top or a countertop. This technique causes the cookies to fall and spread so the edges become a bit thin, wrinkly, and crisp—just like those from a bakery.

**Makes: 2 dozen**

**2½** sticks (1¼ cups) unsalted butter, softened

**1½** cups packed light brown sugar

**½** cup granulated sugar

**1** teaspoon baking powder

**¾** teaspoon baking soda

**1¼** teaspoons kosher salt (Diamond Crystal)

**2** teaspoons pure vanilla extract

**2** large eggs, room temperature

**3** cups unbleached all-purpose flour

**6** ounces semisweet chocolate chips (1 cup)

**5** ounces semisweet chocolate (61 to 66 percent), coarsely chopped (1¼ cups), plus more large, flat pieces for tops (optional)

**1.** Preheat oven to 350°F. Beat butter with both sugars, baking powder, baking soda, and salt on medium-high speed until light and creamy, 2 to 3 minutes. Beat in vanilla. Add eggs, one at a time, beating to combine after each addition and scraping down sides of bowl as needed. Stop beating and add flour, then beat on low to combine. Add both chocolates and beat to combine. (If you are working in a warm room and/or dough feels sticky or soft, refrigerate about 15 minutes before scooping and baking.)

**2.** Using a 2-ounce scoop, drop dough onto parchment-lined baking sheets, 2 inches apart (6 cookies per sheet); press each down to flatten slightly.

**3.** Top each cookie with a few large, flat pieces of chopped chocolate if desired. Bake one sheet of cookies 9 minutes; remove from oven and bang sheet on stovetop or counter to deflate. Return to oven and bake 3 minutes; remove and bang again, then return to oven and bake until golden around edges and just barely set in centers, about 3 minutes more.

**4.** Transfer sheet to a wire rack and let cool 5 minutes, then transfer cookies to rack with a spatula; let cool completely. Repeat with remaining sheets, one at a time. Cookies can be stored in an airtight container at room temperature up to 3 days, or frozen up to 2 months.

# Brownies

*Easy to make and bake ahead, brownies are always welcomed by my guests. I like to top them with vanilla ice cream and hot fudge sauce for an unexpected surprise at a dinner party. The characteristics of an ideal brownie are chewy edges, a fudgy interior (the fudgier the better!), and a crackly top. But you can control the balance of those qualities in the following ways.*

**For extra-gooey brownies:** Bake them in an 8-inch square pan instead of a 9-inch one, knowing you'll have fewer edge servings.

**For easier removal:** Butter the baking pan and line with parchment, leaving a 2-inch overhang on two sides; butter the parchment. The parchment "handles" will aid in lifting the whole brownie slab from the pan after baking.

**For more chewiness:** Replace 3 tablespoons of the butter with a neutral-tasting oil (recognizing that the taste will be slightly less lush).

**For more chocolate flavor:** Cocoa powder provides deep richness, while chopped chocolate creates lovely melty pockets when added in two batches—melt two-thirds with some of the butter and whisk into the batter, then fold the remainder into the batter just before baking.

**For a balanced crumb:** In this recipe, eggs are the only leavening, so adding them one at a time to the batter allows them to be incorporated and offer a bit of a lift.

**For a shiny shell:** Thoroughly whisk the eggs into the still-warm melted chocolate mixture for a good 45 to 60 seconds.

**For molten centers:** Remove from the oven when a toothpick inserted in the middle comes out with crumbs on it—a couple of minutes less than the recipe's bake time.

**For easier cutting:** Let cool in the pan on a wire rack for 20 minutes, then lift them from the pan and allow to cool completely on the rack before cutting into squares.

**Makes: 16**

**1** stick (½ cup) unsalted butter, cut into pieces, plus more, softened, for pan

**¾** cup unbleached all-purpose flour

**2** tablespoons Dutch-process cocoa powder

**¾** teaspoon kosher salt (Diamond Crystal)

**8** ounces semisweet chocolate (61 to 66 percent), chopped (about 2 cups)

**1½** cups sugar

**3** large eggs, room temperature

**2** teaspoons pure vanilla extract

**1.** Preheat oven to 350°F. Butter a 9-inch square baking pan and line with parchment, leaving a 2-inch overhang on two sides; butter parchment.

**2.** In a medium bowl, whisk together flour, cocoa, and salt. In a large heatproof bowl set over (but not in) a pot of simmering water, combine 1½ cups chocolate (6 ounces) and the butter; heat, stirring, until melted. Remove from heat. Immediately add sugar and whisk 10 seconds. Add eggs, one at a time, then vanilla; whisk vigorously until glossy and smooth, 45 to 60 seconds. Using a flexible (silicone) spatula, stir in flour mixture until just combined, then fold in remaining ½ cup chocolate (2 ounces). Transfer batter to prepared pan, smoothing top with spatula.

**3.** Bake until top is shiny and crackly and a tester comes out clean, about 35 minutes. Transfer pan to a wire rack and let cool 20 minutes. Using parchment overhang, lift brownies from pan. Let cool completely on rack before cutting into squares. Brownies can be stored in an airtight container at room temperature up to 2 days, or frozen (as a whole or in individual portions) up to 3 months.

# Pound Cake

*A traditional pound cake calls for just a few ingredients—a pound each of butter, sugar, eggs, and flour, adding up to a rather dense result. I like to incorporate other ingredients, such as leaveners and sour cream, to lighten it up a bit. The addition of vanilla or lemon zest or juice imparts a wonderful flavor. Unlike when making cheesecake, many people consider a crack down the center a desirable hallmark. Heed these tips when following any delicious pound cake recipe.*

**Mixing:** Thoroughly creaming the butter and sugar and beating in the eggs (a bit at a time) are essential for the cake to rise.

**Leavening:** Baking powder yields a cake with a fluffier texture than the classic pound cake. Add it during the creaming process (versus mixing it into the dry ingredients, per the usual method) to ensure it is fully distributed into the batter.

**Prepping:** Pound cakes have long baking times and can get too dark in thin or dark-colored loaf pans. Instead, use a light-colored, heavy-gauge aluminum or aluminized-steel pan. To ensure the cake turns out easily, thoroughly coat the inside of the pan with softened butter, using a soft-bristled brush to reach into the corners; then dust with flour, tapping out any excess.

**Baking:** Starting at a higher oven temperature (usually 325°F to 350°F), then dropping it down (300°F to 325°F) gives the cake a jump start, then allows it to bake slowly so it doesn't turn too brown on the outside.

**Timing:** Given their dense batters, pound cakes often suffer from undercooking, causing them to collapse during cooling. Use three methods to test for doneness: The sides should be pulling away from the pan, a skewer inserted near the center should come out with only a few moist crumbs attached, and the top should spring back when lightly pressed in the center. Continue baking in 5-minute intervals as needed.

**Makes: one
8½-by-4½-inch loaf**

**2** sticks (1 cup) unsalted butter, softened, plus more for pan

**1½** cups unbleached all-purpose flour, plus more for dusting

**1¼** cups sugar

**1** teaspoon baking powder

**1** teaspoon kosher salt (Diamond Crystal)

**2** teaspoons pure vanilla extract

**4** large eggs, room temperature, lightly beaten

**⅓** cup sour cream or full-fat plain Greek yogurt, room temperature

**1.** Preheat oven to 350°F. Butter an 8½-by-4½-inch loaf pan; dust with flour, tapping out excess. Beat butter with sugar, baking powder, and salt on medium-high speed until very light and fluffy, about 6 minutes. Scrape down sides of bowl, then beat 1 minute more. Scrape bowl again, then beat in vanilla.

**2.** Add beaten eggs, a bit at a time, beating well after each addition. Reduce speed to low and add half the flour, then sour cream, then remaining flour, beating until just combined after each addition. Remove bowl from mixer and use a spatula to get all the way down to bottom, stirring and folding to ensure all the butter is fully incorporated. (This will prevent butter streaks on the top of your cake.) Scrape batter into prepared pan.

**3.** Transfer pan to oven, reduce temperature to 325°F, and bake until top is golden and a tester inserted in center comes out clean, about 1 hour 5 minutes. Transfer pan to a wire rack and let cool 1 hour, then invert cake onto rack, turn top-side up, and let cool completely. Slice to serve; or store, unsliced, in an airtight container at room temperature up to 3 days; or freeze, wrapped in plastic, up to 3 months (thaw to room temperature before serving).

# New York Cheesecake

*Of all the many iterations of cheesecake, the iconic New York–style is a classic—rich and dense but not too heavy. The ingredients are rather straightforward—lots of eggs and cream cheese (and often sour cream) in the filling and graham crackers, butter, and sugar for the crust—so you really need to pay attention to the technique. Mastering the method is worth it, since cheesecakes are adaptable in terms of flavor and presentation, and can therefore be served year-round and during the holidays. These tips will help you steer clear of common pitfalls, so you wind up with a (crack-free) cheesecake that looks as pretty as it tastes.*

**For easy unmolding:** When assembling traditional springform pans, you can invert the bottom so the raised lip faces down. This way, you can just run an offset spatula between the pan bottom and the crust, then gently slide the cake onto a serving platter.

**For an even crust:** Use the bottom of a dry measuring cup to press gently but firmly over the cookie-crumb mixture in the pan, including in the corners.

**For a silky-smooth filling:** Take care to bring the cream cheese, eggs, and sour cream to room temperature (about 30 minutes) before blending.

**For a balanced taste and texture:** Sour cream is often added to help offset the denseness of the batter and provide subtle tartness.

**For even baking:** Cooking the cheesecake in a water bath ensures even baking, so the center doesn't crack; not opening the oven door during baking is important, too. The water bath also produces a cake with the creamiest consistency. To do this: Wrap the springform pan in a double layer of heavy-duty foil to prevent water from seeping in, then place in a roasting pan (or deep baking pan). Place it on the center rack of the preheated oven, then fill the larger pan with enough boiling water to come halfway up the side of the cake pan.

**For serving:** To make clean slices, dip a thin-bladed knife in warm water and wipe it clean between cuts.

**Serves: 12**

**6** tablespoons unsalted butter, melted, plus more, room temperature, for pan

**15** graham-cracker sheets (each 3 by 5 inches), broken into pieces

**⅓** cup packed dark brown sugar

**1** teaspoon finely grated lemon zest, plus **1** tablespoon fresh juice

**1¼** teaspoons kosher salt (Diamond Crystal)

**2½** pounds cream cheese (five 8-ounce packages), room temperature

**1⅓** cups granulated sugar

**5** large eggs, room temperature

**1** cup sour cream, room temperature

**1** teaspoon pure vanilla extract

**1.** Preheat oven to 350°F. Assemble a 9-by-3-inch springform pan (as described, left). Butter pan. In a food processor, finely grind graham crackers. Add melted butter, brown sugar, lemon zest, and ½ teaspoon salt; pulse until mixture resembles wet sand. Press evenly into bottom and halfway up sides of prepared pan. Bake until golden and set, 12 to 15 minutes; let cool completely.

**2.** Reduce oven temperature to 325°F. Beat cream cheese on medium speed until smooth. Gradually add granulated sugar and beat until light and fluffy, 2 to 3 minutes. Beat in lemon juice and remaining ¾ teaspoon salt. Add eggs, one at a time, beating well after each addition. Beat in sour cream and vanilla until smooth.

**3.** Place pan in the center of a double layer of foil. Lift edges of foil up, wrapping tightly around sides of pan and folding under until flush with top of pan (this will prevent moisture from seeping in). Pour filling into pan (it should come almost to top of rim); smooth top with a small offset spatula.

**4.** Place filled pan inside a roasting pan and transfer to center rack of oven. Carefully pour enough boiling water into roasting pan to come halfway up sides of springform pan. Bake until cake is puffed, golden brown, and slightly wobbly in center, 1¾ to 2 hours (it will continue to cook as it cools). Carefully remove springform pan from roasting pan; transfer to a wire rack and let cool 20 minutes. Remove foil and run a paring knife around sides of pan to loosen. Let cool completely. Drape pan loosely with plastic wrap and refrigerate until cold, at least 8 hours and up to 3 days. Unmold cake and serve.

# Rhubarb-Strawberry Pie

*I've long favored this combination, in part because rhubarb and strawberries are among the first fruits I harvest from my own garden each spring. Their natural balance of tartness and sweetness needs little embellishment, especially when baked beneath a woven crust that is both functional (allowing steam to escape in the oven) and beautiful—and likely easier to achieve than you may think. It's a recipe you'll return to year after year, and one that belongs in every baker's repertoire.*

**Filling:** Strawberry mellows out the sharp edges of rhubarb, which is why they are a classic pie pairing. You can use raspberries instead of strawberries, or omit berries entirely and increase the rhubarb to 2 pounds total.

**Rolling:** Turning the dough as you roll prevents it from sticking to the work surface and ensures a more even round; keep a dry pastry brush handy to remove any excess flour during and after the process.

**Topping:** When creating a lattice crust, work methodically—folding and unfolding alternating strips as you go—to keep the weave even and the pattern neat.

**Chilling:** Once the pie is filled and the lattice top assembled, chill it in the refrigerator for at least 30 minutes to help the dough hold its shape in the oven.

**Baking:** Cook the pie thoroughly—the fruit juices should be bubbling in the center and the top and bottom crust should be nice and golden, which is why using a glass pie dish is highly recommended.

**Cooling:** Allowing the pie to fully cool, preferably overnight, will yield clean slices rather than a runny filling. The flavors also meld and deepen as the pie rests.

**Storing:** The pie can be kept at room temperature for up to 2 days.

## Serves: 8

### For the filling

**1¼** pounds rhubarb, cut into ¾-inch-thick pieces (6 cups)

**6** ounces strawberries, coarsely chopped (1 cup)

**1½** cups sugar

**¼** cup cornstarch

**¼** teaspoon finely grated orange zest, plus

**1** tablespoon orange juice

Kosher salt (Diamond Crystal)

### For the crust

**2** disks Pâte Brisée (see page 62)

Unbleached all-purpose flour, for surface

**2** tablespoons unsalted butter, cut into pieces

**1** large egg, lightly beaten, for egg wash

Sanding sugar, for sprinkling (optional)

**1.** Preheat oven to 375°F. Make the filling: Mix together rhubarb, strawberries, sugar, cornstarch, zest and juice, and ¼ teaspoon salt.

**2.** Make the crust: Roll out 1 disk pâte brisée to a ⅛-inch thickness on a lightly floured surface. Fit dough into a 9-inch pie plate. Pour in filling; dot top with butter. Refrigerate while making top crust.

**3.** Roll remaining disk pâte brisée to a ⅛-inch thickness on a lightly floured surface. Cut into at least fifteen ½-inch-wide strips using a fluted pastry cutter.

**4.** Lay 8 strips across pie. Fold back every other strip, and lay a horizontal strip across the center of the pie. Unfold folded strips, then fold back remaining strips. Lay another horizontal strip across pie. Repeat folding and unfolding strips to weave a lattice pattern. Repeat on remaining side.

**5.** Trim bottom and top crusts to a 1-inch overhang using kitchen shears, and press together to seal around edges. Fold edges under, and crimp as desired. Refrigerate for 30 minutes.

**6.** Brush crust with egg wash, and sprinkle generously with sanding sugar. Bake pie on middle rack, with a foil-lined baking sheet on bottom rack to catch juices, until vigorously bubbling in center and bottom crust is golden, about 1½ hours. (Loosely tent with foil after 1 hour if crust is browning too quickly.) Transfer pie to a wire rack, and let cool for at least 2 hours (preferably longer) before serving.

# One-Bowl Chocolate Layer Cake

*I have always been a baker, making cakes for birthdays and other special occasions ever since I was a child. A celebration always deserves a wonderful cake. This one is so easy because it's made all in one bowl. Whenever you need a quick and incredible chocolate cake, you can rely on one-bowl "pantry cakes" that use cocoa powder and oil and are mixed by hand—they can be baked in layers, as cupcakes, and in sheet pans alike.*

**Texture:** Using oil, not butter, yields a super-moist cake with a tender, delicate crumb that feels light and fluffy (like in your childhood memories).

**Taste:** If you want to allow the chocolate to shine through, stick to neutral-flavored oils, such as canola, sunflower, or grapeseed oil. For richer flavor notes, you can use a fruity olive oil, which works especially well in chocolate cakes. Also, cocoa powder has plenty of intensity without needing to add chocolate.

**Mixing:** Whisk all your dry ingredients together in your mixing bowl to evenly distribute the baking soda and cocoa powder, then whisk in the wet ingredients until combined.

**Prepping:** Brush both pans well with softened butter. A lot of chocolate cake recipes call for dusting the pans with cocoa powder, which won't be visible on the dark cake after baking; but the cake will be frosted, so you can use flour instead, tapping out the excess.

**Cooling:** This cake is extra moist and prone to sticking, so turn the layers top-side up after inverting them onto the wire rack.

**Frosting:** When making the frosting, be sure to sift the confectioners' sugar to remove any lumps (whisking doesn't always do the trick). A medium- or coarse-mesh sieve works even better than an old-fashioned sifter. And when coating the cake layers, don't skip the "crumb coat" step; this initial thin layer captures loose bits of cake so none of them end up in the final layer of frosting.

### Serves: 12

Softened unsalted butter, for pans

**1½ cups** unbleached all-purpose flour, plus more for pans

**1½ cups** sugar

**¾ cup** Dutch-process cocoa powder

**¾ teaspoon** baking powder

**¾ teaspoon** baking soda

**1¼ teaspoons** kosher salt (Diamond Crystal)

**2** large eggs, room temperature

**¾ cup** low-fat buttermilk, room temperature

**¾ cup** hot tap water

**2 teaspoons** pure vanilla extract

**6** tablespoons vegetable oil

Chocolate Frosting (recipe follows)

**1.** Preheat oven to 350°F. Butter two 8-by-2-inch round cake pans. Line with parchment and butter parchment. Dust with flour, tapping out excess. In a large bowl, whisk together flour, sugar, cocoa, baking powder, baking soda, and salt. Whisk in eggs, buttermilk, hot water, vanilla, and oil.

**2.** Divide batter evenly between prepared pans. Bake until tops spring back when lightly pressed, about 30 minutes. Transfer pans to a wire rack; let cool 15 minutes. Invert cakes onto rack, remove parchment, then turn top-side up; let cool completely.

**3.** Spread 1½ cups frosting over top of one cooled cake layer. Top with remaining layer. Spread a thin coat (about 1 cup) of frosting over top and sides of cake to create a "crumb coat." Refrigerate about 20 minutes, then frost top and sides of cake with remaining frosting.

### CHOCOLATE FROSTING
**Makes: about 5 cups**

In a bowl, sift together 3 cups **confectioners' sugar**, ⅓ cup **Dutch-process cocoa powder**, and a pinch of **kosher salt**. In another bowl, beat 8 ounces **cream cheese**, room temperature, and 2 sticks (1 cup) **unsalted butter**, softened, on medium-high speed until smooth. Reduce speed to medium-low; gradually add cocoa mixture and beat until combined. Pour in 12 ounces **bittersweet chocolate** (about 70 percent), melted and cooled slightly, in a slow, steady stream. Add 1 cup **crème fraîche** or sour cream, room temperature; beat until combined. Frosting can be refrigerated in an airtight container up to 5 days; bring to room temperature and beat before using.

# ENTERTAINING

It has been more than four decades since my very first book, *Entertaining*—which was just recently reissued last fall. When I wrote it, a truly comprehensive, practical, and inspiring guide for home entertaining did not exist, and after years of catering, I firmly believed I was the right person at the right time. I wanted to show that entertaining did not depend on pomp or show but on thought, effort, and care. I also wanted to encourage readers to develop their own entertaining style, reflecting their personal tastes and creativity.

Those same motivations continued to shape the entertaining stories I shared in my magazine *Living* and on my television shows over the years, with ideas for all types of gatherings—cocktail parties, brunches, formal dinners, casual outdoor events, and holiday celebrations. While trends have come and gone, the tenets of good entertaining remain the same: Preparation is key. Organization and advance planning—down to the shopping list and cooking timeline—allow everything to flow smoothly and for everyone to have a good time.

Being prepared also means having the right supplies. I have by now built a very substantial collection of plates, bowls, glassware, and serving pieces, often choosing them by color—drab, whites, soft creams, or pieces rimmed in blue or patterned just enough to be interesting. And I have table settings for every occasion: At Thanksgiving, I serve turkeys on turkey platters and all the vegetables in autumnal dishware. If you are just starting out, I recommend investing in the best white or neutral-hued dishes your budget allows and buying enough to serve your usual number of guests. (Minimalists—including my daughter, Alexis—appreciate this approach, too.) Having a matching set—from flat and round bowls for soup to cappuccino and espresso cups—means you are literally set for anything.

Of course, food and drink are at the heart of every gathering. One of my secrets to successful entertaining is serving a really good drink made with the freshest ingredients and the highest-quality spirits, presented in a beautiful glass. I learned this years ago when I catered events several times a week. Likewise, it is important to choose meals that are tried-and-true and widely appealing. I carefully plan menus to balance variety, timing, and seasonality, building a repertoire of favorite recipes that I can rely on time and time again and that guests look forward to.

Thoughtful planning matters just as much when hosting overnight guests, from assigning rooms in advance to ensuring all their needs are met. My goal has always been the same: for guests to leave well-fed, well-cared-for, and happy.

Remember, too, that being a gracious guest is as important as being a generous host. I never arrive empty-handed, often bringing gifts for the host from my farm—such as beautiful, fresh-laid eggs from my chickens, arranged in a striking pattern based on their shell colors: dark brown from the Marans and the Araucana blue and the Araucana green.

Entertaining—and being entertained—this way brings me enormous joy, and it's a pleasure you can easily make your own.

# 1

# BE PREPARED WITH HOSTING ESSENTIALS

Think of entertaining as one friend treating another friend. The rules and regimens for how you do it are very personal—there's no one proper behavior or one standard of taste. Starting with some basic supplies will make it easier to create a scene that is uniquely your own. Choose items that will make hosting feel effortless and elevated, and evoke an individual sense of style.

**Dishware:** Invest in quality dishware in timeless patterns and shades. Have at least eight of each of the following: salad, dinner, and dessert plates, as well as wide, shallow bowls (for, say, soups and risottos). Build on this cache depending on how often you host and for how many guests. You can even mix and match the dishware for added interest.

**Flatware:** Buy plenty of forks, spoons, and knives, including the different sizes—salad versus dinner forks, teaspoons versus soup spoons, and butter versus steak knives. Individual pieces and sets are readily found at flea markets and tag sales at affordable prices. Try to amass both classic and modern flatware in a range of finishes, along with informal (such as "bistro" styles) and formal options to suit all occasions.

**Glassware:** Frequent hosts will want to have at least six to eight of each of the standards: white wine, red wine, champagne flutes or coupes, and rocks and highball glasses. Fine crystal glasses add sparkle and elegance to holiday meals and special occasions. Because these pieces can be costly, it often makes more sense to accumulate them over time, building a collection that expands naturally and holds memories. (See page 183 for more on crystal collections.) European-style tumblers and stemless goblets are all-purpose alternatives for more casual gatherings.

> ▸ **MARTHA ENTERTAINS**
>
> For washing glass and crystal that is well maintained, use a mild dish soap and a soft sponge. For pieces that have developed tannin and lime deposits, add some white vinegar. Always hand-wash your delicate glassware. The dishwasher could cause breakage, and the typical detergents used are too harsh. It's very important to rinse with warm water—not hot, not cold, as extreme temperatures can cause cracks or breakages. Whenever washing anything delicate in the sink, I like to line the bottom of the sink with a towel, just in case the object slips or accidentally hits the surface. After rinsing, dry immediately with a clean, lint-free towel to prevent spotting. As the pieces are washed, place them on a dry towel next to the sink. I always save old hand towels just for such chores.

**Beverage servers:** Pretty pitchers and carafes are helpful for replenishing water glasses at the table or for serving batch cocktails like Mary's Knees and my signature Martha-ritas. Punch bowls are not only the traditional choice for all manner of punches, from summery fruit concoctions to warm cider punches in the fall, but also for festive mixes like eggnog throughout the holiday season. The bowls can also be filled with greenery and other decorative elements to create arresting centerpieces.

**Table linens:** An assortment of quality linens will open up opportunities for setting a beautiful table. Runners are a nice alternative when you don't want a full tablecloth. Fabric napkins are preferred for brunch and dinner parties, while patterned paper ones are well suited to an outdoor cocktail hour, pool party, or barbecue.

**Serving pieces:** Have a variety of attractive bowls and platters in different shapes and sizes—with at least one of each generously proportioned. Choosing a palette, whether blue (opposite) or otherwise, will ensure your tablescape is coherent. Of course, a wooden cutting board can also double as a cheese or charcuterie board.

# 2

# PLAN A MEMORABLE MENU

The temptation to impress when having people over for drinks or a meal is understandable, but it's worth taking a cue from seasoned hosts, who prefer to rely on a roster of trusted dishes they can depend on. At the same time, entertaining is an opportunity to introduce your guests to something new, whether by tweaking a classic recipe, incorporating an unfamiliar flavor, or mastering a new dish inspired by travel or your personal history.

**Think seasonally.** Share what's growing in your gardens and at your local farmstands, and build a menu to showcase these crops. Feature what's fresh at the market, knowing that peak-of-season ingredients can turn even simple preparations into something much more delicious. A seasonal menu also accommodates varying appetites, with lighter salads, chilled soups, and pastas in summer, and heartier stews and roasts in colder months.

**Think practically.** Now is not the time to try a complicated recipe, at least not without having completed a few test runs beforehand. It is also not the time to attempt too many elaborate dishes. Instead, keep the menu simple, factoring in the number and availability of the ingredients, the cooking methods and times, and whether the dishes need to be served right away. For example, I often turn to my reliable favorites—gougères and cheese straws (at right) for appetizers; honey-mustard salmon, tomato tart, or pasta limone for entrées; and usually something tangy and lemony for dessert.

> ▸ **MARTHA ENTERTAINS**
> Because I like to cook for large groups of people, mussels have become a regular part of my repertoire; they are so very, very easy to prepare and serve. To cook 6 pounds is really not much more difficult than to cook 3 pounds—just double up on the big, covered kettles or spacious skillets. At my house in Maine, it is not atypical to start a luncheon with big steaming bowls of moules marinière, subtly flavored with white wine, a bit of heavy cream, and chopped parsley, basil, or chervil. I often follow that with a grilled half of a steamed lobster swathed in a shallot beurre blanc and a colorful salad of greens and herbs from the garden. Another easy favorite is black pepper mussels—pristine mussels, freshly ground black pepper, and olive oil!

**Think ahead.** Prioritize dishes that can be made at least partially in advance, leaving you with little to do at the last minute. At a summer grilling party, you can have the starters, salad, and dessert ready to go, and then cook the meats to each guest's liking during the event. For an indoor gathering, you could invite guests to sit at the kitchen counter while you finish cooking, letting them help carry plates to the table.

Since my first book, *Entertaining*, in 1982, I've been presenting dips and spreads in beautiful hollowed-out cabbage heads from my garden. To serve the accompanying vegetables for crudités, wrap single large cabbage leaves around glass vessels, and secure them with twine.

**Get creative with your menu.** Simple does not mean boring. Come up with personal twists to make dishes interesting and that your guests will enjoy—such as an almond and grape gazpacho for a refreshing (and equally traditional) alternative to the more familiar tomato version, or an updated risotto made with farro in place of the usual rice.

> **▶ MARTHA ENTERTAINS**
> I like to serve shrimp cocktail on cake stands of varying heights (shown opposite). I arrange the shrimp in rings and garnish each display with leafy green butter lettuce—or whatever else I have growing—from my vegetable greenhouse.

**Consider food sensitivities.** It's always a good idea to ask guests about any food allergies or other dietary restrictions in advance whenever possible; if that is impractical or you are unsure, try to offer at least one or two gluten-free, nut-free, dairy-free, and vegan options that everyone can enjoy.

**Presentation is key.** Decide how the food will be served. Will it be a formal seated dinner where everything is plated in the kitchen? Or a more convivial family-style arrangement with the various components passed around the table? A refined but relaxed buffet-style grazing station works equally well at holiday open houses and other special celebrations (such as rehearsal dinners) or even smaller gatherings throughout the year. Then be sure to select dishes that are well suited to that serving manner.

> **▶ MARTHA ENTERTAINS**
> I love the idea of hosting a holiday brunch, where neighbors and friends stop by and children can accompany their parents. I have a true open house in that guests can go wherever they want on the farm. This is not so different from what my parents did in our family home in Nutley, New Jersey. I always serve a delicious fresh seafood buffet of oysters and shrimp, accompanied by a bar stocked with icy-cold whites, a delectable rosé, and a sparkling wine or two. When preparing this type of spread, I use only the highest-quality seafood sourced from a reputable fishmonger. I always try to find an expert to shuck oysters at my party, but it's easy enough to do it ahead on your own. I also make traditional toppings; I think they taste just a bit better than anything you can buy.

**Don't underestimate dessert.** It's the finale to the meal and what most guests will remember best. While a single showstopper, such as a beautiful lemon meringue pie or crepe cake (at left), can be impressive on its own, consider setting up a help-yourself dessert table with a few different selections—fruit crumbles, brownies, and a tart. Another option is to combine the typical after-dinner coffee and dessert by serving the classic Italian treat called affogato (literally, "drowned"), made by pouring freshly brewed espresso over scoops of vanilla gelato, as shown below.

▶ **MARTHA ENTERTAINS**

I am always rethinking dessert, and though I've never been a big consumer of plain ice cream on its own, I am a longtime fan of affogato, sundaes, banana splits, and ice cream sodas. I started serving "embellished" ice cream at informal dinner parties and discovered that everyone loves digging into a delicious combination of ice cream and flavorful toppings and other components. Personally, I love strawberry shortcake. I adore Key lime pie. And an Almond Joy bar right out of the freezer is a great way to cool down on a hot summer day. Take the basic ingredients of these three delectable favorites—butterscotch and strawberry sauces, lime curd, rich pound cake, crunchy shortbread, and chocolate-almond-coconut clusters—add a scoop or two of high-quality vanilla ice cream, and you have a delightful dessert for a summer dinner party or an afternoon barbecue.

# 3
# BE THOUGHTFUL ABOUT THE BEVERAGES

One of my secrets for entertaining is making a really good cocktail with fresh ingredients and the highest-quality alcohol, served in a beautiful glass. This can set the mood for any party and get an evening off on the very right foot. Focus on simple, straightforward recipes that are universally loved, and personalize them with a twist.

**Stock up on basic bar supplies.** This includes a corkscrew/bottle opener, a cocktail shaker and strainer, a jigger, a muddler, and short tongs for ice. A citrus peeler and bamboo picks are good for preparing and serving garnishes. In lieu of a standard ice bucket, bottles can be chilled in an attractive bowl or other vessel filled with ice. Specialty ice-cube molds are also fun to have on hand. And of course, having a variety of beautiful glasses—coupes, flutes, goblets, rocks, highballs, and tumblers—will ensure the drinks make an impression.

**Serve signature drinks.** Not only is this a great way to limit the number of spirits you need to purchase, but it also acts as a conversation starter—especially if it's an original recipe or a clever update on a popular formula. Keep them cohesive with the season. Spritzes suit warmer months, as do rosé sangria with strawberries and nectarines and yellow watermelon margaritas (shown on page 97); punches, mulled wine, or whiskey-based drinks (such as whiskey sours, opposite) feel right for colder months.

**Provide a DIY beverage station.** If you're hosting a large gathering and want to accommodate all drink preferences, consider designating a help-yourself bar area, with a trusted cocktail book or recipe cards for guests to refer to when serving themselves. Or enlist a friend to be a stand-in mixologist.

> **▶ MARTHA ENTERTAINS**
> Having guests wait in line at the bar during a party is a huge no-no. The answer is premade drinks. For example, when I serve my signature Martha-tinis, I put an ice ball in each glass ahead of time, then pour in the vodka and add the orange slices as the guests arrive. For caipirinhas, another favorite of mine, I mix the drink and fill the glasses well ahead of time, adding ice at the last minute. Pitcher drinks are another great option. I premix a big batch of cider bourbon cocktails in autumn, using my own pressed apple cider.

**Buy enough.** Often, particularly at dinner parties, all that's called for is wine and beer. In these cases, it's a good idea to buy at least one white, one red, and either a rosé or a sparkling wine, depending on the time of year and the menu. For beer, lagers and amber ales are generally food-friendly and universally liked, and there are many locally made craft beers to choose from.

**Consider non-drinkers.** Be sure to offer a few alcoholic-free options, such as ginger beer, kombucha, or flavored seltzers. There are also many excellent alcohol-free beers available these days, as well as nonalcoholic spirits for crafting wonderful mocktails—or simply omit the alcoholic components of your favorite drinks for all to enjoy.

# 4

# GET ORGANIZED AND PLAN AHEAD

The secret to being a successful host is to eliminate the guesswork and anticipate potential problems from the outset. Throwing a party is not difficult, but it does usually involve multiple moving parts. Being organized and planning ahead are simple but critical steps.

**Write out the menu.** Once you've settled on your menu, it helps to write it out. Even if you aren't planning on making menu cards for your guests, you can use this tool to keep you on track. It is all too easy to forget one component—or an entire dish—in the preparation stage and especially during the party. Having the menu in writing means these accidents never need to happen.

**Streamline the shopping.** Make a consolidated list of ingredients needed for all drinks and food being served—going to the store once will save you much time and effort, so be thorough. Account for any specialty items that might need to be ordered online, as well as cooking tools that might need to be replaced.

**Decide what serving dishes will be used.** Doing this as soon as you've chosen the menu will afford you enough time to search your existing inventory and either buy (or borrow) the necessary platters, serving utensils, and other pieces, or invent a creative solution using items you already have on hand.

**Devise a detailed cooking timeline.** Plan the order in which you'll make each dish on the menu, working backward from when they will be served. Note any special make-ahead instructions, such as storage and heating times. See the chart on page 101 for a general guide.

**Consider the cleanup in advance.** Make a plan for clearing the table—preferably never while guests are still seated. Start by emptying the dishwasher and sink and putting away other items before guests arrive, leaving the counters free of all but what's needed. Then designate an area of the kitchen for storing dirty dishes during the party, filling different tubs with soapy water for soaking flatware, fragile glasses, and stacked plates and bowls.

> ▸ **MARTHA ENTERTAINS**
> When I entertain, I fill a plastic basin with soapy water. When the table is cleared, the napkins get presoaked before stains set in.

# Devise a Scheduled Countdown

What this includes will vary depending on the type of gathering, but the following is a good starting point for a brunch or dinner party.

## Secrets to Success

### ▶ A MONTH BEFORE

☐ Send out invitations.

☐ Begin thinking about the mood you'd like to set at the table—formal or relaxed, seasonal or celebratory.

### ▶ THREE WEEKS BEFORE

☐ Choose the menu and make the shopping lists.

☐ Decide on the centerpieces and other table decor.

☐ Decide on your table scheme (linens, china, glassware, flatware).

### ▶ TWO WEEKS BEFORE

☐ Purchase wine, beer, and other beverages.

☐ Take inventory of serving pieces and table accessories such as platters, pitchers, and candleholders, noting anything that needs to be borrowed, purchased, or refreshed.

### ▶ A WEEK BEFORE

☐ Follow up with guests who have not RSVP'd.

### ▶ TWO TO THREE DAYS BEFORE

☐ Prepare make-ahead dishes.

☐ Decide on floral arrangements or other table accents. Trim greenery, condition flowers, and set aside vases or vessels.

### ▶ THE NIGHT BEFORE

☐ Set the table completely, including linens, place settings, centerpieces, and candles.

☐ Prep all produce for the remaining dishes so the kitchen stays calm the next day.

### ▶ THE DAY OF

☐ Chill the wine and beer, light candles shortly before guests arrive, and follow your cooking timeline—leaving yourself free to greet everyone with ease.

# 5

# CREATE AN INVITING SCENE

Even for a casual get-together, your guests will appreciate being in a stylish and comfortable setting. This extends beyond the dining table to the overall ambiance of the space. Here are some guidelines to help you establish the right tone for every event.

**Set a beautiful tablescape.** It doesn't take much to make it captivating, but the table should reflect your personality and convey the desired mood. Laying out attractive place settings will elevate any dining experience. How you go about setting the table depends on the following.

▸ For informal parties, you can stick with the standard six-piece setting: dinner plate, wine glass, water glass, fork, knife, and spoon. Tablecloths are entirely optional, though patterned ones (or runners) can lend personal style.

▸ For formal meals, a crisp white cloth (with the creases ironed out) is still the default, as are cloth napkins in a neutral palette.

▸ It's a good idea to designate seats whenever there are eight or more guests. Besides helping the party run more smoothly, handcrafted place cards contribute visual interest.

**Rethink the centerpiece.** A massive floral arrangement in the middle of the table has its merits, but there are a multitude of other ways to enhance your tablescape, particularly for casual affairs. Consider choosing a single seasonal flower and displaying various varieties of it at different heights (at right).

**Pick a palette to unify the elements.** This could include a monochromatic play on a favorite color, weaving varying shades throughout for added dimension. Or you could choose a bold mix of complementary hues—the combination of dark indigo and bright orange is especially timeless.

Neutral dishware provides a soothing canvas for brightly colored blooms, here displayed in different vessels and at different heights for a more interesting display. Subtle touches, like the gold rimmed glasses and plates, elevate the setting, while mixing gold with silver feels modern.

**Consider other areas.** While the table is typically the focal point and where guests will spend the most time, you'll want to explore opportunities to enhance their experience and extend the hospitality beyond the table. The following details will ensure guests feel considered, comfortable, and quietly impressed from arrival to farewell.

▸ Dim the lights and set unscented candles throughout the home for a warm glow.

▸ Style the entryway to create a good first impression: Clear clutter, add a floral display, and ensure coats and bags have a designated place.

▸ Layer on the comfort in sitting areas with additional pillows, floor cushions, and throws.

▸ Place fresh hand towels, soaps, and other welcome touches in bathrooms.

▸ Create a playlist that reinforces the mood without interfering with conversation.

▸ Adjust the thermostat so the room feels comfortable once guests arrive—spaces often warm up quickly when full.

**Decide on a theme.** A unifying theme—seasonal, botanical, or inspired by a place or occasion—is essential to creating a tablescape that is intentional and cohesive. It also streamlines decision-making so you don't overdo, keeping the scene elegant and balanced. For a nature theme, you could set out assorted vessels filled with a dramatic mix of greenery and simple blooms, arrange moss interspersed with smooth stones and votives down the middle, or collect pretty twigs and leaves for a fall-inspired effect.

▸ **MARTHA ENTERTAINS**
Faux bois, a major theme at Skylands, is often incorporated into the table settings at parties during the summer—such as green faux bois tablecloths, woodland arrangements created in some of my antique French containers, and the menu cards, place cards, and table cards printed with faux bois patterns (shown opposite).

# 6

# BE AN ATTENTIVE HOST

The best food, drinks, and atmosphere will never compensate for an absent or anxious host. It starts with choosing the right menu and avoiding too many last-minute tasks, and it continues by mindfully observing and interacting with your guests. After all, the ultimate goal of any party is to spend time in the company of others.

**Greet guests.** You are the host and ideally should be the one to meet every person at the door and invite them into your home. Doing so conveys a gracious first impression and sets a welcoming tone—particularly if they have brought a thoughtful gift or if they're entering an unfamiliar space. If you're hosting a large event with people coming and going, make an effort to engage with everyone at some point.

**Aid with mixing and mingling.** Unless your guests already know one another, you will need to take the time to introduce them to everyone else, thinking ahead of time about possible prompts to help spark initial connections. Continue to observe the situation throughout the event, stepping in (tactfully) as needed to promote conversation.

**Be physically present.** Do not keep disappearing to the kitchen to tend to the meal. It is perfectly fine to slip away to toss the salad, stir the stew, check on the roast, or brew the coffee, but these moments should be limited in number and time (ideally no longer than 10 minutes a pop).

**Do not rush the food.** A good host allows the meal to unfold at a leisurely pace. Choosing dishes that can sit for a short period before serving is essential for following an unhurried pace, as is waiting until everyone is finished eating before moving on to the next course.

**Help guests get home safely.** Establishing an end time helps ensure your guests leave without overstaying their welcome. That said, you are responsible for seeing them to the door and thanking them for coming (and bringing a gift). Depending on the occasion, you will want to have party favors to share with your send-off.

## 7

# KEEP GUESTS ENTERTAINED

For parties of any meaningful duration, take the pressure off yourself by planning activities that will encourage socializing and truly show your guests of all ages a good time.

**Invite guests to play along.** Lawn games are an integral part of the summer parties at the farm in Bedford, where a level space of land is reserved to play croquet, as well as bocce ball, badminton, and horseshoes. Making apple cider—with an apple press or a food processor—and scavenger hunts are fun fall activities. Provide a firepit to keep everyone warm. Cards and board games like Scrabble are indoor options year-round. All are excellent icebreakers that promote mingling and quick bonding.

> ▸ **MARTHA ENTERTAINS**
> Every autumn, after we pick all the delicious apples around my farm, we make cider using my American Harvester double-tub press. My grandchildren love participating in this fun event! It takes a lot of muscle to grind the apples, so everyone on the farm takes turns. Of course, instead of a traditional press, you could also puree sliced apples in a food processor, then drain them in a cheesecloth-lined colander.

**Tie the activity to the holiday and season.** Doing so makes the gatherings feel special and immersive. Think egg-dyeing and hunts at Easter, a s'mores station and DIY confetti balloons (in lieu of fireworks) on Independence Day, and of course, pumpkin carving for Halloween. Invite people over for tree trimming, cookie baking and decorating, and caroling during the Christmas season.

**Set up a designated table for kids.** When hosting Thanksgiving and other multigenerational gatherings, it's a good idea to cover a small table with kraft paper and provide crayons for doodling and drawing while waiting for the meal to be served and the grown-ups to finish eating. Having a play area with age-appropriate toys, puzzles, books, and games is also highly recommended, as is hiring a babysitter—or delegating the duty to an older sibling—for lengthier events. Besides keeping children engaged, it also fosters independence.

# 8

# HOST HOUSEGUESTS WITH EASE

Hosting houseguests is as much about the food as it is the company—thoughtful meals turn a simple visit into a memorable experience, all without adding stress to your plate. Creating a safe and welcoming environment is equally important.

**Be prepared with some trusted recipes.** Gather a file or a notebook of recipes that are simple and yet still send a message that you care enough to take the time out of your busy life to prepare them. Also, keep a log of who you served each one to, so you don't repeat yourself (unless upon request).

**Look to locally available foods.** Integrate the specialties of the regional, state, and local communities into your menu—it's really what everyone wants to savor when venturing to different areas. Examples include sour cherries in Michigan, wild salmon in Washington state, blue crabs in Maryland, Hatch chiles in New Mexico, and lobster and clams in Maine.

**Plan and shop for meals in advance.** A very important part of a weekend with guests is developing easy but interesting menus, using your cache of dependable recipes. Once the menus for the weekend are set, make shopping lists and buy everything you need.

**Stock the pantry.** Be sure to keep some dependable and interesting ingredients on hand for impromptu snacks and suppers—imported tuna packed in oil; bottarga (dried, pressed mullet roe), which can be stored for months in the freezer; a variety of olives; the best canned anchovies; cured meats and assorted cheeses; delicious crackers and crispbreads; dried fruits and nuts; and seasonal fresh fruit.

**Plan for early risers.** Even if you are intending to serve a communal morning meal, it's a good idea to have some homemade granola, yogurt, fresh eggs, and other breakfast items—such as a streusel coffee cake (at right) that can be prepared the night before—in case guests want to fend for themselves. Setting up a coffee and tea station with all the fixings (and instructions for using any specialty equipment written out) will also make people feel at home.

> **▶ MARTHA ENTERTAINS**
> At Skylands in Maine, I like to make substantial breakfasts for guests because that meal invariably precedes or follows a long hike. For lunch, I keep it simple with self-serve sandwiches or a Niçoise salad. This leaves room for more elaborate dinners that lead to lots of lingering.

**Take inventory of essentials.** Provide extra phone and tablet chargers, put nightlights in bathrooms and hallways, check batteries in safety detectors, replace any burned-out light bulbs, replenish your first-aid kit, and order more firewood and gather kindling. Stock guest bathrooms with plenty of toilet paper rolls and cotton balls.

**Do a safety check around your house.** Even if you've already done this for your own family members and pets, it is wise to take additional precautions to protect any unsuspecting visitors, such as by removing all hazardous items, installing safety gates at the top or bottom of stairs, and blocking any openings in the front or back yard.

**Ready the guest rooms.** Do a thorough cleaning the day before people arrive, changing the bed linens, fluffing the pillows, and providing extra blankets and sleep pillows. A small fan is a nice touch in warmer months. Plush robes and slippers are appreciated any time of year, as are refillable water bottles or carafes, reading material, and a lamp on the bedside table.

> **▶ MARTHA ENTERTAINS**
> To prepare your home for weekend visitors, set out small arrangements of freshly cut flowers in guest rooms. I like to keep it simple with small bouquets of whatever is blooming. Choose a color combination that is unexpected but also understated, such as 'Chocolate Cherry' black sunflowers and chartreuse foliage—a ground cover called creeping Jenny (shown below).

**Offer welcome kits.** Greet each guest with an attractive basket or bin filled with personal toiletries (a toothbrush and toothpaste, a hair dryer, hand soaps, and travel-size bottles of shampoo, conditioner, and lotions). Tuck in a few healthy snacks to tide them over, as well as brochures, maps, and local magazines to acquaint them with the area.

**Offer an introductory tour.** Besides showing visitors to their guest room, this is an opportune time to walk them through your home, pointing out special features (such as the library with books you think they would like), all entrances and exits, home-security alarms (with the codes), fire safety equipment, and an "information station" with Wi-Fi and streaming passwords and instructions for using TV remotes and audio equipment. Be sure to cover outdoor areas, such as a swimming pool, outdoor shower, walking paths, and sitting areas amid your gardens.

**Keep guests engaged and entertained.** Overnight guests will appreciate a range of planned activities that are unique to your hometown, such as an easy hike or horseback ride with a packed picnic, planned water sports like paddleboarding or kayaking, visiting nearby museums, going to U-pick orchards, attending a concert or theater performance, and exploring some of your local restaurant and shopping stops.

**Provide farewell packages.** Send each guest off with provisions (edible and otherwise) for the ride home, along with any collected keepsakes. Handcrafted souvenirs—homemade pickles or preserves with custom labels, potted herbs or plants from your garden, embroidered potpourri sachets, whatever your passion or hobby—are by far the very best way to remind them of their stay.

# HOME ORGANIZING

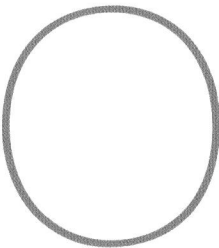

Organizing and homekeeping have always felt instinctive to me—less a learned skill than something intrinsically woven into my every day.

Given my many roles and responsibilities, I could not possibly manage my very busy schedule—both personal and professional—without a well-tended calendar. Each January, I begin a new one by scheduling all health and wellness appointments for the year, then continue to fill it with important to-dos, meetings, and other dates as they arise. My monthly calendar is updated and printed out every week for a thorough review to include all responsibilities—from podcasts and speaking engagements to personal dinners.

An organized calendar—one in which every meeting, trip, and appointment is thoughtfully recorded and timed—allows me to accomplish a great deal each day. I adopted this practice in my twenties while juggling the demands of work, marriage, and young motherhood, and it quickly became essential for keeping track of everything and enjoying it all. By the time I launched *Living*, I knew I wanted to share this personal organizing tool with readers. In 1992, we began publishing "Martha's Calendar" in each issue, offering travel plans, birthdays, and other personal items not found in other calendars. It resonated with readers immediately and became one of the magazine's most popular features.

I am equally committed, of course, to keeping my home organized and running smoothly. The kitchen is the hardest-working room in my home, and I have developed and discovered many strategies over the years to improve its efficiency and enjoyment. Open shelves keep everything accessible, while customized storage ensures every inch is used wisely—even otherwise overlooked spaces. And the less used pots, pans, and baking supplies get relegated to the basement, stored on industrial racks, with like items grouped together.

When you embark on your own organizing and homekeeping projects, I encourage you to take the lessons in this chapter to heart—especially tackling only one room at a time to avoid feeling overwhelmed, and giving everything a home to prevent clutter and chaos. The checklists included here will help you stay on top of routine cleaning and maintenance, and, like my own calendar, can be adapted to your particular home.

# 1

# FOCUS ON ONE ROOM AT A TIME

An organized home calls for having a system in place—and sticking to it. This thoughtful, proactive approach will benefit you in the long run, leaving you free to spend more time and energy on activities that prove meaningful to you. Too often, organizing efforts are derailed by the prospect of addressing an entire home at once. But that's generally unrealistic without the help of a professional. For a more manageable approach, spread out the tasks over time. Incremental victories will keep you motivated and on track.

**Start with high-traffic, high-reward areas.** In most homes, these include the kitchen and bathrooms, with playrooms another troubleshooting space for growing families. Pick the one that gives you the most bother, and do not move on to the next until you are satisfied with your efforts. Also, if organizing the whole kitchen is too overwhelming, break it down into sections—focus on (for example) the island and cupboards one day and all the shelves and drawers on another, saving the pantry for its own session.

**Pare down your belongings.** Before you begin, set up a process for sorting the contents of each space into three boxes, labeled "keep," "donate," and "sell." Don't overthink it. If you haven't used, worn, or otherwise touched an item in the past year, it's probably not worth keeping. Look for charitable organizations in your vicinity that accept household goods and apparel (check their websites for accepted donations). There are many ways to sell items of value as well, including tag sales, consignment shops, and online platforms. Try to minimize what goes in the garbage to promote sustainability and to avoid adding to landfills.

**Rethink your current storage.** Now that you've whittled down your belongings, it's time to reevaluate how to accommodate them. You may already have the means to do this, such as by repurposing a piece of furniture—a chest that once held extra throws can now store toys in a kids' room, or a rolling cart can be relocated from the kitchen to a bathroom or home office. The ultimate goal? Provide a home for everything.

> ▶ **MARTHA ORGANIZES**
> I love baskets of all different kinds. The oldest-known baskets have been carbon-dated to between 10,000 and 12,000 years old. Over the years, I've collected a number of them from auctions, antiques fairs, and tag sales, or from the talented basketmaking artisans themselves. Some of my baskets are antique; some more contemporary; some were used during my catering days. I've collected hundreds, so when I moved to my Bedford farm, I had a small structure built to house them (shown opposite), which is located near my grove of bald cypress trees across from my clematis pergola. Every so often, I like to clean and organize this basket house so the beautifully handmade containers remain in good condition.

# 2

# GIVE EVERYTHING A HOME

Things have a way of staying where you put them. The secret to an organized home, then, is to channel this truism in making sure wherever you put "it" is where it belongs—and not just left on the dining table or kitchen counter in a rush, only to take up permanent residence there. This fundamental approach in organization makes spaces more intuitive, reduces visual clutter, aids in identifying duplicates for decluttering, and simplifies maintenance.

**Store it where you use it.** To embrace this common-sense principle, the next time you find something without a home, identify which room it belongs in. Then come up with a storage solution in that area, ideally right away.

**Create purpose-based stations.** For a multitasking space, you could designate bill-paying, personal correspondence, and crafting zones, stashing the supplies for each in separate (labeled) cubbies. Mini stations in a laundry room could include stain-fighting solutions, mending supplies, and tools for ironing and steaming.

**Group like with like.** Sorting all your wooden cooking utensils into one crock and metal ones into another not only makes sense functionally, but it also looks better. In a closet, this could mean grouping clothing by type (shirts, slacks, skirts, and dresses) or by color. In a bathroom, you could store all lotions in one spot, hair products together, and cleaning supplies separately. For a kids' room, consider having all stuffed animals on one shelf and puzzles and games on another.

**Think in multiples.** Storing different items in matching containers instantly makes a space more orderly and visually appealing. This trick works exceptionally well in concealing all the different toiletries and makeup products in a bathroom, which are often eyesores.

**Decant staples.** This simple step helps save space and create a more curated look. By using clear containers, you can see when supplies are running low, such as powdered detergents and other products in a laundry room, and dry goods (beans and legumes), dried spices and herbs, oils and vinegars, and other nonperishables in a pantry or the refrigerator (such as your own salad dressing). Decanting pet kibble into a tightly sealed bin not only looks neater but will also keep it fresher longer.

**Keep certain items in open view.** When the objects being stored are aesthetically pleasing, you can display them. Think of beautiful bowls on open shelving in a kitchen, gardening implements on a pegboard in a shed, or cherished art books on a coffee table. No space in your linen closet (or no such closet at all)? Hang beautiful throws and blankets on a Shaker-style peg rail, and stack Turkish towels on a wall-mounted rack above the tub.

**Put underused space to use.** The above suggestions help you maximize a bare wall for additional storage, but you can also leverage the areas underneath beds, tables, and other furniture pieces, using coordinated bins and baskets that blend in with the room's décor. Organizing products, such as over-the-door racks, drawer inserts, and shelf risers, also help make the most of every inch.

# 3

# CUSTOMIZE STORAGE FOR COMMON TROUBLE SPOTS

Forget about finding a one-size-fits-all organizing solution, which simply doesn't exist. Instead, tailor your approach to each room's contents, focusing on the following problem-prone areas. Pick the one that gives you the most angst before moving on to others.

**Organize the kitchen.** To have a truly functional kitchen, the path to efficiency depends on the size and layout. But the "golden rules" of organizing always apply, including using every inch—the larger the kitchen, the greater its contents—as well as giving everything a home. The following key steps will enable you to achieve this worthwhile objective.

▸ Keep countertops clear. It's perfectly fine to keep a few items out that you use regularly. I keep my cappuccino machine in one area and a collection of mortars and pestles in another, with bowls of fresh eggs handy. Just be sure you have ample room to work so you don't have to spend time rearranging before each cooking session.

▸ Add an island. A kitchen island expands your counter space and provides a central spot to prep and sometimes eat. Putting it on wheels allows for greater flexibility in case you need to move it out of the way. Make sure you have the right-size island for your kitchen, allowing at least 3 feet around the island when possible. A too-big island will only make maneuvering in the kitchen more difficult. Also, try to find (or design) an island with built-in storage below; you can also mount hooks on the sides for hanging dish towels or aprons.

▸ Strategize the storage. As daunting as it may sound, emptying all your drawers, cabinets, cubbies, and shelves will give you a fresh start, allowing you to rethink your organization and really upgrade it in one fell swoop. Once you've done this, follow the three-box rule on page 122, and decide what you want to keep, donate, or sell. Next, sort the items into categories—for example, baking supplies, serving pieces, everyday dishware and flatware, miscellaneous utensils, pet supplies, and cleaning products. Then you can figure out the best place to keep each category.

▸ Keep items where you use them. Store pot holders, cooking utensils, and pots and pans near the range, and aprons, knives, cutting boards, and a compost bin within arm's reach of the island or other prep area. Ideally, plan to house your everyday flatware, glassware, and dishes in proximity to the dishwasher and sink. Less frequently used items can go above the refrigerator, in the bottom drawers, or behind more basic supplies in cabinets. Designate a drawer for miscellaneous cooking utensils and another for odds and ends (aka a "junk drawer"), and reserve deep shelves for platters, books, and pet supplies, and small cubbies for towels and other items.

▶ Mine every inch. Expand your kitchen footprint vertically, whether by installing a hanging pot rack to free up cabinet space or utilizing wall space with floating shelves, over-the-door solutions, magnetic strips for knives, and pegboards to keep utensils and tools off your counters and out of drawers. In addition, use adjustable shelf risers, vertical dividers, and other cabinet organizers to stretch the storage capacity, tuck lidded bins in a space above upper cabinets, and add hooks and racks to walls or inside cabinets for hanging items. Adding drawers to the empty space under lower cabinets is yet another way to sneak in more storage, such as for a foldaway step ladder.

▶ Employ open storage. Replacing upper cabinets with open shelving can make your kitchen feel lighter and airier, but this arrangement consistently requires more careful curating of the contents. Limit what you display to everyday essentials and pieces you truly love—think neatly stacked plates, frequently used glassware, and a few well-chosen serving bowls. Group like items together and keep quantities modest to avoid a cluttered look. Finally, leave a bit of open space between groupings; negative space is key to maintaining a calm, polished appearance. Corral like items into coordinated bins and trays; bamboo or woven materials lend warmth and texture, or consider painting basic options to match the overall color scheme.

> **▶ MARTHA ORGANIZES**
> My dogs spend a lot of time in the kitchen with me. When we head out for walks, it's usually through the kitchen door, so I keep their sweaters and coats in a basket on a shelf under the island. A shallow drawer keeps coiled leashes from getting tangled. My cats have their own buffet in the servery. The dishes are lined up in a long tray, which catches any spills, so food doesn't end up on the floor.

**Streamline the pantry.** Organizing your pantry makes cooking easier, reduces waste, and saves money by keeping everything orderly and easy to access. Aim to do this every three to six months. Here's how to do it efficiently:

▶ Take inventory. Toss all expired goods, then sort the rest into "stations" such as dry goods, baking supplies, canned goods, and snacks. Stack multiples so you can see what you have at a glance. Also, store items due to expire first in front of those with later "best-by" dates.

▶ Decant staples. Store dry goods—grains, beans, nuts, and other items—in clear vessels for a streamlined appearance and so the contents are visible. For eco-friendly decanting, upcycle larger jars (such as for store-bought sauces) and, if desired, spray-paint the lids' exteriors (leaving the interiors unpainted) with two coats of Rust-Oleum paint in your desired shade, letting them dry in between. Put your pretty bowls and crocks to use by consolidating snacks in them.

> **▶ MARTHA ORGANIZES**
> When decanting dried pasta, beans, and rice and other grains into jars, note the basic cooking instructions on a piece of paper cut to fit inside the lid or under the bottom, taping it to adhere. For example: Bring 1 cup pearl barley + 3 cups water to a boil. Simmer, covered, 45 minutes. This way, even guests can help themselves.

- Group like with like. Corral like items into coordinated bins and trays; bamboo or woven materials lend warmth and texture, or consider painting basic options (such as wooden crates) to match your color scheme.

- Add labels. You can put stickers on each container, or designate zones (such as for oils and vinegars, condiments, and breakfast items) and attach bookplates or other labels to the shelving underneath.

- Utilize a door. For a walk-in pantry, hang a tiered rack over the door to house canned goods and other small items, or mount shallow floating shelves for a similar result.

**Bring order to the laundry room.** Take a two-step approach to keeping this utility area tidy and efficient. The first step is to explore ways to utilize the vertical space around the machines. The second is to contain all the supplies. For small spaces, the key is to incorporate storage for greater functionality.

- Think vertically. Opt for custom built-in (or store-bought) cabinets that fit around your washer and dryer, creating side shelves and overhead storage. Install open shelving to store items like laundry soaps, stain removers, brushes, and paper towels, putting seldom-used supplies on the top shelves. Attach Shaker-style pegs or hooks to the shelves or walls to hang brooms, laundry bags, and dustpans for easy accessibility.

- Contain the supplies. Tuck assorted items into coordinating bins and baskets to lend the space a polished look. Replace bulky (and unsightly) boxes of detergent and other supplies with refillable, clear containers to create a more streamlined and organized appearance. Designate specific bins for different categories of items, such as one for detergents and fabric softeners and another for sewing needles and buttons.

- Maximize a small footprint. If you have a front-load washer and dryer, stacking them can free up floor area and open up options for custom cabinetry and shelving. You can also mount door racks or shallow shelving on the back of the door to store smaller items without taking up valuable floor or shelf space.

- Have a stain-fighting kit. Store all the ingredients in their own bin: isopropyl alcohol, hydrogen peroxide, acetone, white vinegar, diluted dishwashing soap, enzyme detergent, and mineral oil.

> **▸ MARTHA ORGANIZES**
> Many years ago, I created a stain removal chart (shown opposite) that has continued to be a dependable resource for common culprits while also evolving over the years. Bookmark the chart on pages 150–151, or laminate a copy to hang in your laundry room.

**Systematize the closet.** An organized closet doesn't just look good. It saves you from the chaos of searching for that dress or accessory at the last minute and can even prevent you from spending excess money, so you don't end up buying duplicates or pieces you don't actually need. A first critical step is to purge unwanted pieces; it may seem overwhelming, but it can be completed in a weekend. Then you will find it far easier to implement a system for organizing the contents—and keeping them in check. If you have a sizable wardrobe but limited storage space, consider working with a closet organization company.

▸ Empty the space. There's no getting around this preliminary exercise. Pull out every single item to get a clear visual of the closet area and account for your wardrobe, making it easier to go through them.

▸ Evaluate the items. Employ the three-box rule: one for items you want to keep, another for items you plan to donate, and a third for items that aren't fixable and need to be repurposed (such as using old T-shirts as cleaning rags). Pay special attention to any pieces you have not worn in the last year or no longer fit well. If you are struggling with letting go of certain items, enlist the help of an impartial friend.

▸ Sort the items. Once you've settled on the clothes and accessories you're keeping, group like with like (such as shoes and boots, swimwear, and workout gear) to help you determine how many items you have in each category.

▸ Size up the space. With nothing in your closet, measure how much hanging, drawer, and shelf space you have. You can also measure the height of the hanging rods. If this feels overwhelming, then at a minimum, measure the width, height, and depth of your closet shelves and drawers. This will also ensure you purchase storage tools that fit.

▸ Use baskets and bins. These containers allow you to compartmentalize items so they're easier to find. For example, you can have baskets for fitness apparel or beachwear, and clear bins for seasonal sweaters or boots.

▸ Make adjustments. Now that you have your inventory and measurements, you can lower or raise hanging rod heights and shoe shelves (if they are adjustable). Also, place any purchased bins and baskets, dressers, trays, or other storage solutions in your closet.

▸ Put your closet back together. As you arrange your pieces, store items you wear regularly in easy-to-reach places. Likewise, put less frequently used pieces in harder-to-reach places, like a top shelf or back corner. You can organize or style your closet by item type (dresses, skirts, pants, tops, accessories), color, formality, or season—whatever system works best for you.

▸ Buy matching hangers. The best way to create more space in your closet and provide a uniform look is to swap out your mismatched hangers for a coordinating slimline version.

▸ Put every square inch to use. Maximize the space beneath your hanging clothes by placing a shoe bench or a drawer unit on the floor. You might also have room to tuck a smaller dresser here, which will save you space in your bedroom.

▸ Corral accessories. Small organizational trays or drawer inserts help keep jewelry, sunglasses, scarves, and other items from getting lost in the shuffle.

▸ Routinely edit. Tidy up your closet at least once per week, using this time to rehang or refold items or put items back in their place. Use this time to do mini edits, too, to make a seasonal or yearly session less daunting. For example, if you try something on that doesn't fit or has a stain, take action in the moment.

**Tidy the bathroom.** As one of the most frequently used rooms in your home, the bathroom must strike the right balance between form and function. And as one of the smallest, it tends to clutter quickly. A minimalist approach can help streamline your morning and evening routines, boost your mood, and make the bathroom easier to clean.

▶ Edit your inventory. From skincare and hair tools to cleaning supplies, bathrooms tend to fill up with stuff. The surest way to gain drawer space and make your self-care routines more manageable is to reevaluate your products and keep only what you use. In addition, set a timeline for holding on to (and restocking) items, such as six months (after which many skincare products are no longer as effective). Having fewer to dig through—and fewer to replenish—will save you time and money.

▶ Clear the counters. These surfaces tend to function as a depository for everything from toothbrushes to water glasses. Invest in a storage system that will enable you to put everything away as soon as you are finished using it.

▶ Mine the under-sink area. If you have a pedestal sink, you can use that precious floor space to keep frequently used items, such as extra hand towels, toilet paper rolls, and personal care items in a stackable drawer unit or a narrow multitiered rolling cart.

▶ Make use of vertical spaces. Floating shelves can be mounted above a door, tub, or toilet, while more shelves or hooks can be mounted to the inside of the door. Replacing a mirror above the sink with a medicine cabinet is another idea—and the most efficient place for your everyday supplies. A rustic ladder offers a place to hang spare towels.

▶ Categorize items. Have designated drawers for various necessities—such as hair tools, cosmetics, and shower essentials—and add dividers to group your items so they're easier to see and access. For open shelves, sort the items into attractive bins, baskets, crocks, or other storage containers.

▶ Make it personal. Incorporate houseplants, artwork, and other decorative objects to create an inviting environment—and turn the functional space into a mini retreat.

> **▶ MARTHA ORGANIZES**
> I like to keep bath towels and other bathroom linens folded all the same way, so they hang very easily over towel bars and look very attractive. Specifically, I fold them in thirds, then in half, and in half again, organizing them on shelves by size and color so everything—from washcloths to hand towels—has its place.

**Declutter your desk.** Studies show that physical clutter leads to mental clutter, hampering productivity, efficiency, and creativity. Whether you have a dedicated home office or a workspace in the living room or other shared area, it's imperative to create an environment conducive to focusing and staying on task.

▶ Get rid of what you don't need. Paperwork piles up fast. Keep tax documents for seven years and receipts for item warranties (you can even scan and store these items in the cloud). Be ruthless with the rest, shredding anything with personal information to reclaim space in the filing cabinet. Toss outdated planners and desk calendars, along with any productivity "tools" that didn't pan out for you. Also, rehome any decorative object that is distracting.

▶ Centralize your planner. Having multiple planners can create confusion, leading to missed appointments and overlooked key dates. Be sure to sync your digital and paper calendars, too.

▶ Use store-bought organizers. Storing pens, pencils, notepads, sticky notes, and other everyday supplies in a single multifaceted holder not only keeps your work surface clean but also means you never have to search for them. A computer stand raises your monitor or laptop and offers storage underneath. To keep drawers tidy, use inserts to sort similar supplies and personal effects.

▶ Think vertically. Use the wall space above your workstation or elsewhere in the area for shelves and/or an inspiration board. When possible, tuck a filing cabinet or rolling cart under the desk.

▶ Add multitaskers. Choose furniture that serves a dual purpose, such as storage ottomans or desks with built-in file cabinets. Or repurpose a sideboard or armoire for hidden storage in a shared space.

▶ Personalize the space. Use stylish decorative boxes or bins—and even a handsome ladder—to store supplies, display favorite art and photographs, and add potted plants to brighten the space.

# Schedule It In

Once you've put your home in order, you'll want to keep it that way, lest you end up back where you began. The secret is to do a little every day. Here are suggestions for sneaking in tasks during any downtime—or being intentional about squeezing these moments into your daily routine. Set a timer, too, to avoid distractions.

## Secrets to Success

*If you have . . .*

### ▸ 10 MINUTES

☐ Put shoes and toys away.

☐ Wipe down kitchen and bathroom counters.

☐ Tidy up around pet bowls and litter boxes.

☐ Clean out your purse or other carryall.

☐ Organize credit card receipts.

☐ Sort through mail, catalogs, and magazines.

☐ File bills and other documents.

☐ Clear off your nightstand.

☐ Go through your spice rack, noting anything that needs replenishing.

☐ Check your first aid kit and make a list of missing supplies.

### ▸ 30 MINUTES

☐ Organize items in a single dresser drawer or on one closet shelf.

☐ Shred paperwork with personal information.

☐ Sort through your makeup and discard any items that have expired.

☐ Clear your email inboxes and unsubscribe from promotional senders.

☐ Declutter your smartphone by deleting unused apps, outdated contacts, old voicemail messages, and lengthy text chains.

### ▸ 60 MINUTES

☐ Review digital photos, deleting unwanted images as you go.

☐ Reorganize the pantry.

☐ Empty one kitchen cabinet or drawer and organize its contents.

☐ Go through your bookshelves, putting titles back in order.

☐ Clean out your car, including the trunk.

# 4

# ESTABLISH A CLEANING REGIMEN

Having a spotless home is one of life's simple pleasures. With today's busy lifestyles, achieving that worthwhile state can be challenging. The answer? Devise a comprehensive home cleaning schedule by breaking it down into manageable tasks that can be done daily, weekly, monthly, or seasonally. Then you can refer to these checklists and clean your home practically on autopilot. Knowing general cleaning principles will also help.

**Adopt daily habits.** Just a few minutes of daily cleaning can make a significant difference in how your home looks and feels. Plus, it keeps messes at bay so they don't become bigger headaches down the road. Consider tasks that can be addressed from the waistline down, such as your floors and countertops. This is especially important in the kitchen, where surfaces can harbor and spread germs that cause foodborne illness. Start with these simple tasks:

> ▶ **MARTHA ORGANIZES**
> If you're not patient enough to fold a fitted sheet, simply put it back on the bed immediately after laundering it each time.

- ▶ Make the bed.
- ▶ Wipe down kitchen and bathroom counters.
- ▶ Sanitize high-touch surfaces.
- ▶ Wash dirty dishes or load the dishwasher.
- ▶ Put away clothes and toys.
- ▶ Tackle stains on the spot.
- ▶ Wipe the stovetop clean after cooking.

> ▶ **MARTHA ORGANIZES**
> So many people ask me if you really need to clean the stove every time you cook. The answer is, absolutely yes! Wipe it down thoroughly to prevent grease buildup and odors and to maintain the efficiency of your stove. It will also make a deep cleaning that much easier.

**Develop a weekly cleaning routine—and stick to it.** While daily tasks keep your home in check, weekly cleanings go further in targeting dust, dirt, and pet dander, with a focus on high-traffic areas and the most commonly used rooms. Designating the same day of the week for cleaning will help you adhere to the schedule, although some people prefer to spread the chores over two or more days—say, tackling the upstairs on one day and the downstairs the next. The following is a suggested checklist that you can adapt to address your specific needs. The items are listed in the recommended order. Floors always go last.

▸ Launder bathmats, towels, and washcloths.

▸ Clean toilets, bathtubs, showers, and sinks.

▸ Wipe mirrors.

▸ Dust surfaces, including furniture, objects, and light fixtures.

▸ Change and launder sheets and pillowcases.

▸ Fluff pillows and comforters.

▸ Launder machine-washable throw rugs and runners.

▸ Sort through inboxes: Pay bills and file paid bills and paperwork.

▸ Discard magazines and catalogs; store those you want to keep.

▸ Flush the kitchen drain with boiling water.

▸ Wipe the kitchen counter, sink, ventilation hood, refrigerator, and cupboard doors.

▸ Wipe the inside of the oven, microwave, and toaster oven.

▸ Clean the inside of windows and glass doors.

▸ Empty trash bins and wipe the insides and outsides.

▸ Vacuum and mop floors.

**Do monthly deep cleanings.** These sessions target out-of-sight, out-of-mind areas that don't merit weekly attention but, if left unattended for long, could get out of hand. Again, try to choose the same day each month—such as the first Saturday or Sunday—so you won't forget (creating a calendar alert will also help). Below is a sample to-do list. Also, use this time to examine upholstered furniture for stains and tend to any that have gone overlooked.

- ▸ Wipe the insides of medicine cabinets.
- ▸ Scrub the grout in tubs and showers.
- ▸ Wipe the tub and shower surrounds.
- ▸ Launder pillow protectors, mattress pads, and shams.
- ▸ Dust shelves and storage bins.
- ▸ Discard food in the pantry and freezer that's past its prime.
- ▸ Wash the ventilation hood filters.
- ▸ Deep clean humidifiers to remove mineral deposits (following the manufacturer's instructions or by soaking in a diluted vinegar solution).
- ▸ Dust portable and ceiling fans.
- ▸ Flush all drains with vinegar, boiling water, and baking soda.
- ▸ Wipe interior and exterior doors and trim.
- ▸ Clean switch plates.
- ▸ Vacuum fireplace screens.
- ▸ Vacuum window treatments, moldings, and windowsills.
- ▸ Vacuum floors and baseboards.
- ▸ Wet mop floors.
- ▸ Wash the vacuum filter and allow to dry.
- ▸ Buff waxed stone, masonry, concrete, and wood floors.

> **▸ MARTHA ORGANIZES**
>
> When washing the outside of my windows, I like to use a white vinegar and water solution. Vinegar safely kills germs and is much more economical than chemical cleaners. Plus, it's completely nontoxic and antibacterial. Vinegar can strip paint, however, so you'll need to protect the window frames and sills when spraying the windowpanes with the solution. Be sure to also wash storm windows after taking them down and before storing them each spring. Wash exterior windows on an overcast day, as direct sunlight can cause streaking.

**Create a semiannual floor-to-ceiling checklist.** A twice-yearly once-over is crucial for maintaining your home in optimal condition, helping you ward off potential issues and prolong the lifespan of your appliances. Spring and fall are the ideal times to do this, along with other seasonal tasks (see below for more information on those).

▸ Launder pillows.

▸ Rotate and flip mattresses (as needed).

▸ Vacuum mattresses, box springs, and bed frames.

▸ Clean a hanging pot rack and polish copper cookware.

▸ Deep-clean the oven.

▸ Organize and wipe down the pantry.

▸ Empty kitchen cabinets and wipe them clean.

▸ Empty the refrigerator and clean the inside and the bins.

▸ Rotate stacked books to prevent warping.

▸ Clean leather furniture.

▸ Sweep out the fireplace.

▸ Wash the washing machine's filter.

▸ Vacuum the refrigerator and dryer vents.

▸ Vacuum the area behind the refrigerator, washer, and dryer.

▸ Swap out seasonal clothes and store what is no longer needed.

▸ Donate (or sell) clothes you no longer want.

▸ Clean out the makeup drawer and toss expired items.

▸ Clean shower heads and faucet filters.

▸ Vacuum walls and ceilings.

▸ Buff and polish wood floors to restore shine and address minor scratches.

**Adhere to general cleaning principles.** While there is no right or wrong way to clean a home, time-tested practices can enhance the efficiency and effectiveness of the process.

▶ Always clean from the highest to the lowest areas, working from upstairs down and from the ceiling to the floor.

▶ At the same time, start at the farthest point from the door and move to the front of the room.

▶ Clean dry before wet. For example, dust all surfaces in a bathroom and vacuum the floor before cleaning the sink, tub, and toilet. End by wet mopping.

**Minimize dust.** One of the biggest indoor culprits for allergies and asthma is dust mites, which settle into carpets, rugs, upholstery, pillows, and mattress folds, triggering reactions. While it is impossible to eliminate dust entirely, you can significantly reduce its accumulation by taking a few simple steps.

▶ Place natural fiber doormats at all entrances. Do this inside and out—and be sure to wipe your shoes before entering the home. Taking off your shoes will also help contain the dust and dirt.

> **▶ MARTHA ORGANIZES**
> I have always enforced a strict no-shoe policy inside my home, keeping a basket of slippers in various sizes for guests and protective booties for workers to wear over their shoes. Everyone leaves their outside shoes by the door.

▶ Check for leaky windows and doors. These are common passageways in allowing dust (and insects) to enter. Also, avoid leaving windows wide open all the time, especially those on the first floor that face the street. That said, it's fine and refreshing to raise the sashes a couple of inches when the weather is nice, so long as the screens are in good shape.

▶ Change your air-conditioning units' filters regularly. This applies to both central AC systems and window units. Doing so will improve your home's air quality, boost energy efficiency (saving money on bills), ensure your system runs smoothly (preventing costly breakdowns), and extend the overall lifespan of the equipment.

▶ Launder your bedding weekly. Sheets, pillows, and covers collect dust particles that are eventually kicked around your room. Shake throw pillows and comforters outside every so often, too, and air out your bedding every two or three days by pulling back your covers during the day.

▶ Keep pet dander and dirt in check. Wipe your pets' paws when they come inside, brush their coats with a quality deshedding tool daily (outside), and bathe them regularly. Launder their bedding every two weeks, first shaking the covers outdoors to avoid clogging your washing machine. Go over upholstered furniture where they sleep with a lint roller daily, or cover it with washable blankets for easier cleaning.

▶ Run an air purifier. This will help trap the dust before it has a chance to settle on surfaces. Clean or change the filter as directed by the manufacturer.

▶ Invest in a good vacuum. Sweeping just raises the dust, so it's essential to choose the right vacuum for your situation (and budget), learn how to use the attachments effectively, and follow the instructions for maintaining the machine over time. Note: A vacuum with a HEPA filter removes 99.7 percent of all dust particles as well as pollen and bacteria.

▶ **MARTHA ORGANIZES**
Instead of vacuuming and then mopping, the new "wet-dry" machines that vacuum and mop all in one are incredibly efficient and effective. I love the simplicity of the design and how easy it is to clean and use, especially with so many animals and people traipsing through my rooms every day. My house really puts these machines to the test!

# Stain Removal Basics

**The diluted-soap solutions called for below are made with 1 tablespoon of fragrance- and dye-free liquid soap (containing sodium laurel sulfate, or sodium laureth sulfate and 9.5 ounces of water). Pour it into a tiny spray bottle. Do not use the enzyme detergent, also called for below, on protein fibers, such as silk, wool, cashmere, or angora. Always wash fabric after using a dry solvent (such as mineral spirits or acetone), and do not use acetone on acetate. Amodex is a nontoxic cream effective at removing everyday stains, including ink, food, grease/oil, wine, blood, grass, and more from most fabrics.**

| Stain | Treatment |
| --- | --- |
| ▸ **GREASE** (butter, oil, mayonnaise) | Treat area with a dry solvent (such as mineral spirits or acetone) in a well-ventilated room. Using an eyedropper, rinse with isopropyl alcohol; dry well. Spray diluted dishwashing-soap solution on any remaining residue, and soak the item in an enzyme detergent before washing. |
| ▸ **PROTEIN** (blood, egg) | Spray diluted dishwashing-soap solution on stain, and let it sit; rinse in tepid water. If stain remains, treat area with an enzyme detergent, and wash according to label instructions. |
| ▸ **FRUIT OR VEGETABLE** (juice, jam) | Spray diluted dishwashing-soap solution on the stain to remove sugars. Using an eyedropper, rinse with vinegar and then hydrogen peroxide to remove any remaining color. Follow up with an enzyme detergent to remove residue before washing. |
| ▸ **GRASS** | Treat area with a dry solvent in a well-ventilated room. Press with cheesecloth; tamp with a soft-bristled brush. Repeat to remove as much pigment as possible. Flush area with isopropyl alcohol, tamp, and let dry. Follow up with an enzyme detergent to remove residue before washing. |
| ▸ **RED WINE** | Spray diluted dishwashing-soap solution on stain; tamp with a soft-bristled brush. Flush with water, then apply white vinegar and 1 or 2 drops of ammonia to wet area. Flush with water. Treat with an enzyme detergent; wash. If stain is still there, apply a powdered nonchlorinated color-safe bleach, such as sodium percarbonate; rewash. |
| ▸ **WHITE WINE** | Flush the stain with cold water, and spray with diluted dishwashing-soap solution. Treat area with an enzyme detergent and then wash. |
| ▸ **COFFEE OR TEA** | Using an eyedropper, flush area with lemon juice or white vinegar to remove stain; then treat with a stronger bleach, if necessary. To help remove coffee or tea with sugar or milk, spray area with diluted dishwashing-soap solution, then wash with an enzyme detergent. |
| ▸ **CHOCOLATE** | Gently scrape off excess chocolate; spray area with diluted dishwashing-soap solution. Follow up with an enzyme detergent to remove residue before washing. |

| Stain | Treatment |
|---|---|
| ▸ **LIPSTICK** | Use a dull-edged knife to remove excess lipstick. Using an eyedropper, apply a dry solvent (such as mineral spirits or acetone) in a well-ventilated room; tamp with a soft-bristled brush. Flush area with isopropyl alcohol, and tamp. Repeat until all stain is removed, and let dry. Spray with diluted dishwashing-soap solution. Treat with an enzyme detergent, and wash. |
| ▸ **WAX OR GUM** | Use ice to freeze wax or gum, or place item in the freezer; scrape or crack off as much as you can, then remove residue with an oil solvent or mineral spirits. Rinse with isopropyl alcohol; let dry. Treat with an enzyme detergent; wash. |
| ▸ **MUSTARD** | Using an eyedropper, flush stain with vinegar; then wash with diluted dishwashing-soap solution. |
| ▸ **SAUCES** (tomato, ketchup, barbecue) | Scrape off sauce; spray area with diluted dishwashing-soap solution. Soak in tepid water. If color remains, apply white vinegar with an eyedropper. Treat with an enzyme detergent; wash. If color persists, apply several drops of hydrogen peroxide; let sit. Rinse; treat again with enzyme detergent, and wash. |
| ▸ **SOY SAUCE** | Spray with diluted dishwashing-soap solution; tamp with a soft-bristled brush. Flush with water, apply white vinegar, and tamp; let stand several minutes, and flush again. If stain remains, apply hydrogen peroxide, and let stand. If stain persists, apply 1 or 2 drops of ammonia to wet area. Flush with water. Treat with an enzyme detergent; wash. If stain is still there, apply a powdered nonchlorinated color-safe bleach, such as sodium percarbonate; rewash. |
| ▸ **VINAIGRETTE** | First, treat stain as a grease stain (see grease, above). Then flush with white vinegar to remove any remaining spot. Follow up with an enzyme detergent to remove residue before washing. |
| ▸ **FELT-TIP INK** | First, determine whether the ink is oil-based or water-based by building a "dam" around the stain with mineral oil or petroleum jelly using an eyedropper; work within the confines of the "dam." Test the ink with a cotton swab saturated with water and another one saturated with isopropyl alcohol. If isopropyl alcohol pulls more pigment out of the stain, follow the steps for ballpoint ink stains below. If water is more effective, spray the stain with diluted dishwashing-soap solution, then flush with cold water. Alternately, to remove permanent marker, apply Amodex Ink & Stain Remover to the stained area. For fabrics, gently rub with a brush, then rinse or launder. |
| ▸ **BALLPOINT INK** | Build a "dam" around the stain with mineral oil or petroleum jelly. Always work within the confines of the dam. Treat area with isopropyl alcohol using an eyedropper. Remove any remaining pigment with a dry solvent in a well-ventilated room; let dry. Rinse with diluted dishwashing-soap solution, then wash with an enzyme detergent in warm water. |
| ▸ **MUD** | If stain is a combination of mud and grass, treat grass stain first (see grass, opposite). Shake or scrape off residue; pretreat stain with diluted dishwashing-soap solution, and soak. Then treat with an enzyme detergent; wash. |

# 5
# DEVELOP A MAINTENANCE MINDSET

Owning a home requires ongoing diligence, with routine maintenance being the most effective way to avoid costly repairs. Don't leave all the different responsibilities to chance. Instead, devise organizing tools to ensure nothing gets overlooked. Technology is your friend, too; consider using a home maintenance app that will provide a customized preventive schedule and send reminders and notifications.

**Be proactive and prepared.** Preventing problems from taking hold is the best way to protect your investment and your home's inhabitants. Despite all best efforts, some issues will still manage to come up. Then it is a matter of paying enough attention to catch them early on and have a plan for addressing them.

▶ Schedule it in. At the beginning of each year, put all the known homekeeping tasks in your planner, using the checklists in this chapter as a guide.

▶ Establish relationships with reputable contractors—plumbers, electricians, HVAC engineers, roofers, gutter services, and others. Knowing who to call when an emergency arises is key, and many providers will not respond to people who are not existing clients.

▶ Set aside money for future repairs and improvements. A general financial rule of thumb is to contribute 1 percent of your home's value to a dedicated "home maintenance" savings account each year.

> ▶ **MARTHA ORGANIZES**
> In a musty closet, attic, or basement, leave an incandescent light bulb on to dry the air or hang packets of desiccants around the space. Having a dehumidifier and a circulating fan is important for preventing mold and mildew in an unfinished cellar.

**Create a home-organizing log.** It's a good idea to compile all essential homekeeping paperwork and other information in a single binder or a storage bin, clearly labeling it and filing it in a designated "home command center"—such as in the kitchen or a laundry/utility room. Ensure that all members of your family, as well as any regular visitors such as housekeepers, dog walkers, or contractors working on extended projects, are aware of its location.

▸ Keep records. Document all home repairs and service provider information for easy referencing. This can be particularly important if the problem is recurring, indicating a faulty product.

▸ File all owner's manuals, warranties, and registrations. You typically need to refer to the model and serial numbers when scheduling a repair. It's also wise to schedule inspections for any products that are about to expire, so any issues can be addressed (and covered) before the end date.

▸ Make a floorplan. If you don't already have a floorplan of your home, you can check with local county records or create one using a software program. Clearly mark the location of the main gas and water supply shut-off valves, fuses, circuit breakers, or power sources, using color-coded stickers for each utility (or use a digital platform).

▸ Label the mechanicals. Write the name of the water source on a tag and wrap it around the appropriate water pipes. Do the same for the shut-off valves. Check to make sure the circuit switches are also clearly labeled; if not, ask your electrician to do this.

▸ Prioritize safety. Note the location of fire extinguishers and smoke/carbon monoxide detectors, including those in attics or basements. Also, have your fire extinguisher inspected annually by a professional (start by calling your local fire department). Between those visits, look for any dents, rust, leaks, corrosion, or other visible damage that warrants immediate attention.

# Seasonal Checklists

**It's all too easy to let some of these timely to-dos fall by the wayside unless you have a handy reminder sheet to refer to. You can adapt it according to your location.**

| Season | Tasks |
|---|---|
| ▶ **SPRING/ SUMMER** | ☐ Turn on water supply for outside spigots.<br><br>☐ Power-wash the exterior (at least every other year).<br><br>☐ Retouch outside paint or stain as needed (most paint jobs last about 10 years).<br><br>☐ Have any large trees inspected for winter damage, especially those near structures.<br><br>☐ Clean gutters before the rainy season; check downspouts for proper drainage.<br><br>☐ Test the sump pump and clear debris from the exit pipe.<br><br>☐ Monitor dehumidifier in a basement or crawl space to empty basin (or ensure attached drain is working).<br><br>☐ Repair or replace damaged window screens.<br><br>☐ Have HVAC system cleaned and serviced.<br><br>☐ Make needed repairs to driveways, decks, and patios.<br><br>☐ Clean exterior exhaust vents.<br><br>☐ Test water (using an at-home kit, sold online or at home improvement stores) for hardness (i.e., mineral content); install a water softener as needed. |

> ▶ **MARTHA ORGANIZES**
> Use daylight saving time changes as reminders to test smoke/carbon monoxide detectors twice annually—once in the spring when you set your clocks one hour ahead, and again in the fall when you set them back an hour.

| Season | Tasks |
|---|---|
| ▶ **FALL/WINTER** | ☐ Have a pro address any water issues (or mold) in a basement or crawl space.<br><br>☐ Have chimney inspected and cleaned before using the fireplace.<br><br>☐ Flush hot water heater to remove sediment.<br><br>☐ Get gutters cleaned after leaves have fallen; check downspouts for drainage.<br><br>☐ Winterize AC system (or remove and store window units).<br><br>☐ Have your heating system serviced before turning it on; replace any filters.<br><br>☐ Hire a tree service to identify any dead/damaged trees that pose a risk to structures or power lines.<br><br>☐ Relocate liquids that will freeze from a garage or shed.<br><br>☐ Shut off water to outdoor faucets; drain spigots and protect with insulation. |

# COLLECTING

I have always been a collector. One of the first things I started collecting was books. As a child I'd visit our local library, Nutley Public Library, weekly and borrow five to ten books at a time, devouring them as soon as the dinner dishes were done. I began collecting in earnest as a young married mother. Whenever a subject captured my interest—cooking, gardening, landscape design—I sought out as many books on it as I could afford, often combing neighborhood bookstores for titles that promised both beauty and useful knowledge. Collecting was never about owning for its own sake; it was about curiosity and the pleasure of learning deeply. Over time, my shelves filled, not quickly, but thoughtfully, each volume chosen or gifted for a reason.

Soon enough, I began building a gardening library, inspired by the impressive collections at the New York Botanical Garden and the Kew Royal Botanic Gardens in England. I became fascinated by antique illustrated volumes and rare monographs on specific types of plants. With the help of knowledgeable booksellers, I learned how to search for these works as well as nineteenth-century works by Gertrude Jekyll and William Robinson. I gathered twentieth-century texts by English expert Vita Sackville-West and Americans Helena Rutherfurd Ely and Daniel Hinkley. The hunt itself became part of the enjoyment.

Beyond books, I have collected a great many other objects, all intended for use. My Bedford home is filled with copper pots and pans, stoneware bowls, crystal glassware, extensive china dishware, McCoy pottery, and antique furniture, among other cherished pieces. My jadeite collection is large enough to outfit a small chain of diners and spans the full range of Fire-King's iconic milky-green mid-twentieth-century restaurant ware. I have my daughter, Alexis, to thank for sparking this passion during a road trip more than three decades ago. She has no idea how many pieces she owns, and over the years, parts of her collection have found their way to my home (and onto the sets of my television shows, where viewers have fallen in love with them, too). These stunning pieces are incredibly sturdy, which is why so many have survived without so much as a chip. I've even fed my cats out of the small bowls.

When collecting, it is important to acquire with intention. Seek out items that have purpose and lasting value. Collect what you need, prioritizing items that are functional, beautiful, and capable of enhancing daily life. Display them thoughtfully but practically—grouping like items together and maintaining orderly storage systems—so they are easy to access, appreciate, and use every day. Finally, remember that collecting is an evolving practice that keeps both your home and your eye engaged, while quietly connecting generations through objects passed along.

# 1

# COLLECT WHAT YOU USE

Another way of saying this is, use what you collect. There's nothing wrong per se with amassing items based purely on visual interest—for example, vintage typewriters that are no longer operable but can be cleverly displayed on the shelves of a home office or library. However, a common guiding principle is to choose pieces that are not only aesthetically pleasing but also serve some other purpose. And unlike when buying brand-new items, surrounding yourself with your collections makes your home more personal.

**Choose form and function.** Look for items that are practical and useful for your daily life, whether it's a collection of dessert servers (as detailed on page 163), assorted rolling pins, colorful Pyrex cookware (see page 167), white ironstone platters, ceramic pitchers, fruit jars, clay flowerpots, wrought-iron plant stands, or other functional items for indoors and out. Indeed, in these instances, necessity is often what drives the pursuit in the first place.

**Curate items for the home.** Of course, artwork and photography also serve a real purpose, providing beauty or visual interest to your home. The same can be said of other decorative objects, including period furniture (from Queen Anne to midcentury modern), rugs, striped throws and blankets, tole trays, Venetian glass vases, and crisp white linens.

> ▶ **MARTHA COLLECTS**
> When I finally got a house, I started to look at objects as things to gather. I'm still not a serious collector; I am more of an accumulator of interesting accoutrements and tools. And some of those things, such as my cooking and entertaining finds, turn into beautiful collections.

**Start with the basics.** Dishes are a gateway for many people to collect. They're plentiful, available in every price range and imaginable pattern, and leave a clear trail because they're marked with the manufacturer. If you want to see the history of style, manufacturing, and social change in a single subject, it's all right there.

**Indulge an interest in fashion.** Many people collect vintage (and new) handbags, shoes, scarves, and other apparel, as well as jewelry from various eras and styles—all of which can be incorporated into your daily rotation.

**Consider repurposing goods.** Just because you no longer set the table with butter dishes (for example), if you fancy their heritage and beauty, you may want to collect them for another use, such as corralling jewelry, keys, or office supplies. Those same functions can be served by trinket boxes, originally designed to hold cigarettes.

# Dessert Servers

This elegant tabletop tool—defined by its flat and usually triangular blade—is cleverly designed to allow the first slice to emerge intact and as beautiful as the rest. Although commonly known as a pie server, the implement is also used for other baked goods. Some excel at slicing a frosted layer cake; others at easing a tartlet onto a plate. Their diversity of styles and prices is precisely what makes collecting them such fun.

▶ **MODERN MATERIALS** *(shown opposite)*
Early in the twentieth century, the dessert server broke free of the silver cabinet and began to find expression in a variety of materials. The yellow one with the red handle (bottom) is a rarity because it is made entirely of celluloid, which was the first widely used plastic. Celluloid is, however, fragile and flammable—and thus elusive today—so it was quickly replaced by more practical materials, such as Bakelite, which came into use during the 1910s and '20s. Three German servers with two-tone Bakelite handles are shown (right, left, and bottom left). Vivid colors, such as the red (left), increase the value of Bakelite handles. Plastic servers, such as the white one (upper left), were often sold as part of Tupperware sets in the '60s. Ceramic servers, such as the mid-twentieth-century one with a red floral motif (right), were often sold with matching cake plates. They are easily breakable; therefore, they've become particularly rare.

▶ **EMBELLISHED STYLES** *(shown on page 165)*
What unifies these servers from different eras are their ornate blades and handles. Top left quadrant: The server at the far left was engraved using a technique called bright cutting, a practice that originated in eighteenth-century England that involves cutting facets to create a sparkle. Sometimes these decorations were stamped (third from left), while the bold reliefs (fifth from left) were created in a mold. Bottom right quadrant: The subtler decoration on the 1880s server (fourth from right) was created by acid etching using a stencil. Some early-twentieth-century pieces by Scandinavian designers are also shown, including a piece with a rounded blade by Eliel Saarinen (far right) and another with an openwork handle (second from right). Austrian and German servers (such as the third from right) are slender because the pastries and tortes made in those countries tend to be small.

▶ **MARTHA COLLECTS**
Dessert servers sometimes suffer from a case of mistaken identity, as they look remarkably similar to items such as crumbers or jelly trowels. You can usually identify a dessert server by its flat blade and triangular shape. Over the years, cake, pastry, and pie servers have been embellished in many ways; decorative blade edges, however, as seen on three pieces from the twentieth century (page 164), are rare finds.

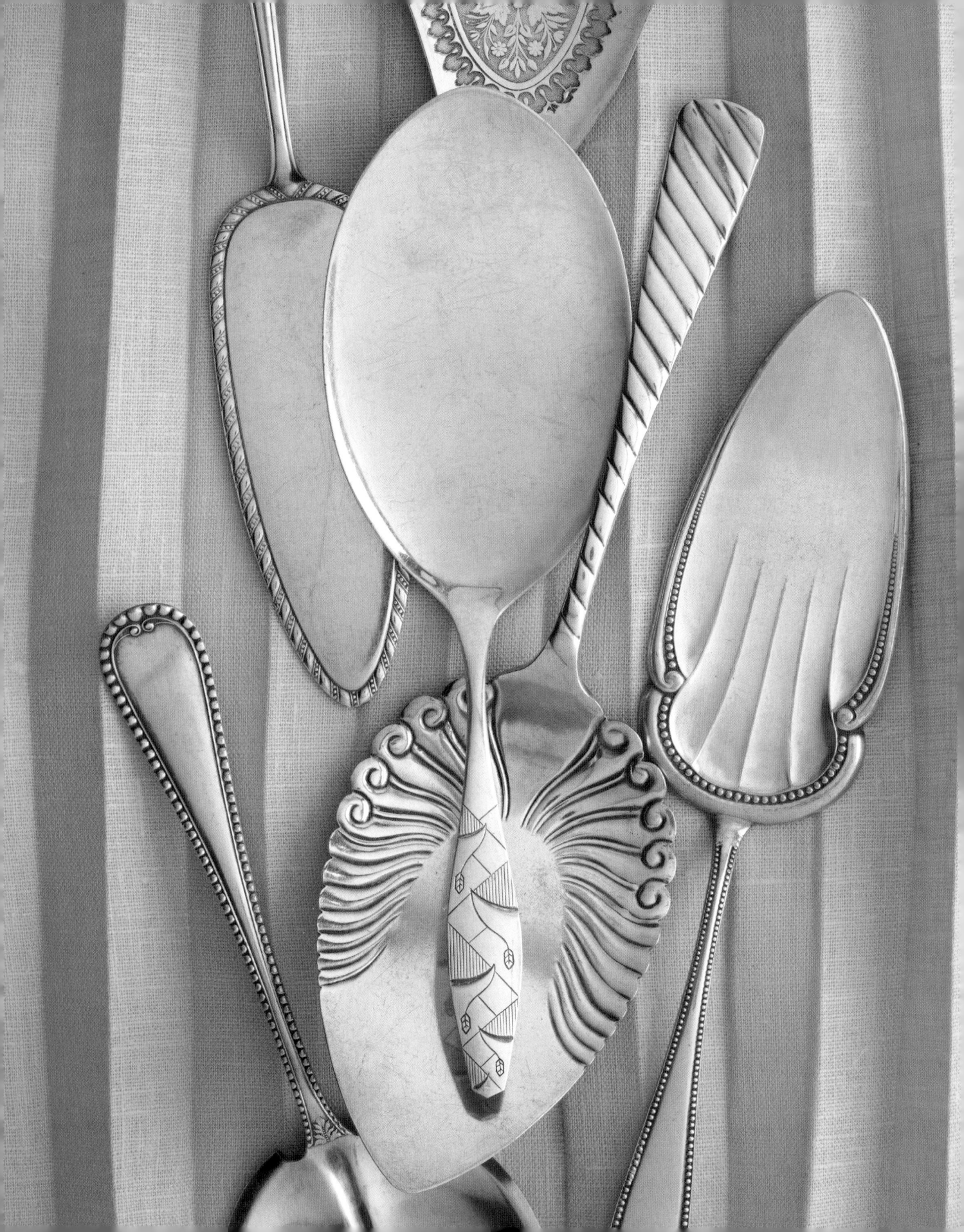

Given the essential (and enjoyable) role cooking has played throughout history, it's no wonder that kitchenware remains immensely popular among collectors. Some celebrate ingenuity—charming pie birds allowed steam to escape from pies, thereby elevating the art of baking—while others are a testament to durability and frugality.

## Eggcups

The earliest known examples of eggcups—designed to hold soft-boiled eggs upright in their shells for easy tapping and peeling—trace to ancient Rome. The tiny vessels remained items of luxury in the medieval and Renaissance periods before mass production during the Industrial Revolution (nineteenth century) made eggcups affordable for the middle classes. The Victorian era saw a surge in variety and design, with eggcups produced in silver, glass, pottery, and novelty shapes. Collecting eggcups, known as pocillovy (from the Latin *pocillum ovi*, meaning "small cup for eggs"), became popular, especially from the twentieth century onward.

## Jadeite

Glassmakers produced occasional jade-green pieces as early as the nineteenth century, but jadeite flourished in the early twentieth century as tastes shifted from post-Victorian ornament to clean, modern color. For the next 25 years it was made by the ton, and much of it survives because it was so well crafted. Thicker, heavier jadeite dishes designed for restaurant use are favored by many collectors. These pieces come in several designs, as evidenced by the shapes of the cups shown here.

### ▶ MARTHA COLLECTS

My collection at Skylands began more than three decades ago, when my daughter, Alexis, started gathering pieces on a cross-country road trip. We've collected every shade of green and nearly every form imaginable.

## Pyrex

In many ways, Pyrex is as practical today as it was a half century ago, when the pieces were favorites of the postwar kitchen, able to go in the oven, refrigerator, and freezer. Pyrex was launched in 1915 by Corning Glass Works of Corning, New York, which still manufactures it. The nesting bowls, double boilers, and au gratin dishes were low-tech and often cost less than a dollar apiece at hardware and department stores. Time was, vintage Pyrex was purchased as replacements for a chipped mixing bowl or passed down by previous generations. But more recently, the cookware has attracted new admirers, particularly among those who grew up with it and appreciate its durability (and nostalgia factor), as well as younger generations who like the iconic midcentury modern design. Collectors especially covet colored Pyrex in pristine condition. For many, the original four-piece nested mixing bowl set (made from 1947 to 1977) remains the signature collectible.

## Enamelware dishes

For many collectors, this throwback dishware conjures vivid memories of cooking over a campfire—or at your grandmother's stove. Its true provenance begins in Germany in the sixteenth century, when the safe, convenient coating made it possible to boil food without causing it to burn. Enameled cookware came to the United States in the first half of the 1800s, with the first speckled products attributed to a company that became known as Nesco. Each plate, bowl, mug, or lidded pot has a shatterproof tin base and a durable porcelain coating, given swirls and bright hues by mixing in minerals. The current lightweight, shatterproof, oven- and dishwasher-safe pieces are as practical as ever. While new enamelware is still being produced today, you can find very nice vintage pieces at thrift shops, tag and estate sales, flea markets, and online at very affordable prices.

## Tourist map textiles

Tourist map tea towels are a mid-twentieth-century phenomenon that emerged from the broader evolution of printed tea towels. Those with state and city maps reached their heyday in the 1950s and '60s, when they were sold in souvenir shops across the nation. Today, these road-tripping mementos make charming decorative elements that can be used as intended or displayed on the wall. The challenge to collecting these isn't their scarcity—there are plenty to go around online—but their condition. They frequently turn up faded and frayed; gentle wear and tear, however, only adds to their character, particularly when they're put to decorative use. The biggest manufacturer was J. H. Kimball; you'll know its wares by the tiny gold rectangular label in the corner.

## Butter dishes

In the late nineteenth century, butter dishes—often known as butter pats—were highly popular, embodying the Victorian ideal of assigning a specific place for every item. These small plates were crafted to complement the stylish dinnerware of the era, such as enamelware, glass, and patterned or plain porcelain. Today, they can bring a unique charm to a festive meal or a dinner party—you can mix different styles and use them as saltcellars. Beyond the kitchen, these versatile dishes have modern applications: The delightful yellow pansy dish, for example, would make a cheerful organizer for jewelry, paper clips, or other small items.

# 2

# CHOOSE MEANINGFUL OBJECTS

Rather than accumulating a collection for the sake of vastness or strictly for value, prioritize items that hold meaning, express your personality, or contribute to your everyday enjoyment. After all, a collection doesn't have to be about how costly or old the objects are. Instead, consider how the collection fits into your life, triggers reminiscences, and forms a narrative about who you are over time. Focusing your collection will also help you avoid accumulating random items.

**Draw inspiration from life experiences.** Think of significant events, travel, or family history you want to explore through objects. For example, your collection could include seashells, rocks, or nautical motifs to remind you of your childhood summers on the beach, whereas items from a specific country or region might harken to your ancestral heritage.

**Identify themes.** Reflect on what you are passionate about, such as culture—art, theater, film, music, and dance are all represented in prints, paintings, and other media—history, nature, or social issues. Vintage decanters, tumblers, and other barware (as shown on page 178) will appeal to oenophiles and home mixologists. Gardeners could collect heirloom implements or botanical-inspired objects; sewers or knitters may want to explore patterns, pincushions, fabric remnants, and other supplies.

> **▸ MARTHA COLLECTS**
> My many travels have influenced my collections. For one example, my trips to Japan have inspired my lifelong interest in the country's culture, food, and cookware. Whenever I'm there, I make a special effort to visit Nishiki Market in Kyoto, where there are more than 125 shops and stalls selling traditional food and ingredients, and Shinmonzen-dori, the street of antiques. Many years ago, I purchased a pair of oversize lacquered kimono trays (one shown opposite) at a huge Japanese flea market. At my home in Bedford, I set them on Chippendale stool bases and use them as side tables.

**Be open to discovery.** A collection often starts with one lucky find. Browse tag sales, flea markets, estate sales, and antiques shops to see if anything captures your attention. Soon enough, you'll have three, five, and more of a kind and can begin branching out from there. The journey is often what gives the items meaning, too—such as where you found them or who you were with.

▶ **MARTHA COLLECTS**

My father, Edward Kostyra, was a fine gardener who lovingly tended our backyard garden in Nutley, New Jersey, including a long hedge of lavender that grew on a rock wall, producing fragrant flowers every year. In 1964, he collected lavender seeds after the harvest and stored them in a small jar labeled with the year. That jar ended up tucked away in an old desk drawer and remained forgotten for decades—until my youngest sister, Laura Plimpton, discovered it in 2014. Curious if they would still grow, I planted some of the seeds in trays in my greenhouse, not knowing if anything would sprout. To my delight, they did—and the plants now flourish in my Bedford gardens, filling the air with the same soft lavender scent that I remember from childhood. In this way, collecting seeds preserves more than a plant—it safeguards a living connection between generations, reminding me to save seeds without knowing who might one day use them.

**Build on what you have.** Odds are, you have already begun accumulating certain objects over the years, be they vintage tea stirrers, candlesnuffers, or crocheted pot holders. Or you can expand on a small, inherited collection from a loved one, such as Bakelite jewelry or swag vases, which you can then research to find similar pieces.

**Narrow the field.** Instead of collecting books in general (for example), limit your scope to a more specific category, such as first editions, illustrated volumes, limited editions, or those on a favorite subject (photography, architecture, women's rights, world history, etc.). A similar approach applies to period furniture, fine china, artwork, and so many other types of collections.

# Brass Objects

With the 1997 purchase of my Skylands house in Maine came the wonderful discovery of beautiful brass pieces, such as trays in an array of shapes and sizes, that looked stunning in the light. So, I continued the tradition of using brass there. Here are some tips for amassing your own brass collection.

## Secrets to Success

### ▸ BUY

When I purchase brass, I don't care where it came from or how valuable it is. If it's appealing to me in shape or size or pattern, I buy it. My assortment has grown beyond those initial trays to include, vases, lamps, buckets, sconces, and more trays from around the world.

### ▸ CARE

Don't worry if some of the pieces (like mine) are severely dull and tarnished—or even almost black—when you find them. Polishing and buffing with brass cleaner (I use Wright's Copper and Brass Cleaning Cream), soft rags, sponges, gloves, and a toothbrush for crevices will have them shining like gold again. It does require elbow grease and time, but the result is worth every ounce of effort.

### ▸ DISPLAY

I don't keep any of the brass pieces in storage. I use everything. The large trays are tables, and the smaller pieces are used as decoration or as flower containers.

### ▸ DISCOVER

You can find a wide selection of brass pieces from around the world at 1stdibs.com. It's especially exciting to find the large trays. Some of them, such as the Indian and Middle Eastern ones, even came with their own stands. I always keep an eye out for them when I'm traveling.

# ▶ FASHION COLLECTIBLES

A sweet cameo gifted by your grandmother or a diamond ring passed down through the generations is an auspicious start to a growing collection. These and other trinkets are often rich in sentimental value and prized for their ability to tell a story. Some pieces may have deep cultural significance, while others allow for personal expression.

## Makeup compacts

Vintage mirrored compacts, once a glamorous must for on-the-go makeup applications, are still readily found and not too precious for everyday use (many inexpensive ones were gifts with a purchase at department stores). They are also pretty enough to feature on a wall in your dressing area or bedroom, where you can pick one to tote along. The selection shown here demonstrates the wide range of materials and styles, including painted enamel compacts with flower motifs, black-and-gold deco, metal varieties, embellished glossy "scales," and midcentury rarities by Chanel and Dior.

## Bakelite

This jewelry was ahead of its time when it appeared in the early 1900s. The material, an almost-indestructible synthetic resin, was first used for car and radio parts but quickly found its niche in fashion. Sculptural and lightweight, it comes in saturated colors that mimic pricier stuff: A shade called apple juice resembles amber, and marble green passes for jade. Basic red and black have always been most desirable, however, even though they're no rarer than other colors. The jewelry went out of production by the '70s, but it spans decades of styles, from art deco to '60s boho.

### ▶ MARTHA COLLECTS

So-called end-of-day marbled Bakelite—the name refers to how the pieces were made by mixing that day's leftover batches together to avoid waste—can command hundreds or even thousands of dollars at auction.

## Cameos

These timeless treasures made their first appearance in Hellenistic times, when they were chiseled into small pieces of stone to immortalize leaders and mythical heroes. More recent versions, like the ones shown here, enshrine anonymous women who were graced with the most desirable traits of their day; the two beauties with light-peach backdrops are from nineteenth-century Italy. Often carved in shell, they were sold to Victorian travelers on European tours, who'd bring them home to wear as status souvenirs. The trend caught on: By the early 1900s, less expensive glass ones were mass-produced to meet demand—that's why you can find vintage profiles, in a range of colors and prices, set into nearly every form of jewelry. What's more, jewelers continue to create modern iterations, keeping them in the style spotlight.

# ▶ BARWARE COLLECTIBLES

Whether you are a serious collector of fine wine or just love hosting cocktail and dinner parties and being a home mixologist, the world of barware is readily available and in a wide variety of uses and price ranges. The following pieces merely scratch the surface. Other options include corkscrews, bottle openers, cocktail shakers, jiggers, muddlers, ice buckets, and coasters.

## Victorian tumblers

Decorated with delicate blooms, these Victorian tumblers—colorful molten glass molded into credit card–thin cups with baked-on lasting hand-painted designs (and sometimes gilded rims)—were first made in the 1800s. Later, companies in Europe and the US followed suit. Unlike Moroccan and Indian tea glasses, which are similar but fluted in shape, and made from clear glass dipped into bright lacquer that can flake over time, Victorian versions are straight-sided. At one time, you could buy sets of six with a pitcher or punch bowl, but they chipped easily, so you're more likely to find singles or pairs now. Most measure about 4 inches tall; cordial glasses (bottom right), just 2—and typically cost less than twenty-five dollars.

## Decanters

Dating to the early twentieth century, colorful decanters were originally used to bring up alcohol from cellar barrels or to disguise inexpensive varieties. Their shape and size speak to what they may have contained and where they're from. Sherry or claret would have been poured into the small ones, while large ones generally held wine. Simple designs, such as the tall purple decanter (bottom right) made by Blenko Glass, in Milton, West Virginia, are typical of American manufacturers; Italian versions, like the green vessel with the finial stopper (top left), tend to be more ornate. In addition to making a serious statement on a home bar, these eye-catchers serve as equally stylish containers for chilled water or a handful of long-stemmed flowers at a dinner party. Look for bottles with their original tops intact, as these will retain their value—and utility—more than those without the matching plugs.

## Tea stirrers

By the late seventeenth century, small spoons known as tea stirrers were being used to blend sugar into tea, a custom that grew with the beverage's rising popularity and availability. The twisted-handle variety has been stirring nostalgic memories for over a century. Before tea bags became common in the 1920s, straw-and-stirrer combos featured tiny perforations to filter leaves while sipping. In that same decade, elegant sterling-silver spoons were sold as chic add-ons to matching flatware sets. By the '60s, Tupperware versions were inexpensive and available in a range of pastel hues. Search online for "vintage iced-tea spoon" and "glass iced-tea straw" to begin—or expand—your own collection.

## Swizzle sticks

Some sport fish fins, others take the shape of airplane propellers, and still others are topped with poodles or flamingos. Vintage swizzle sticks certainly make mixing vodka and tonic more fun, but they were designed as advertising. Every drink served at a hotel bar or on a plane could be a plug for some business. The ones shown here are colorful plastic sticks from the 1950s and '60s, which you can bring out at parties. Buy them in bulk—they are practically a dime a dozen—at flea markets and vintage shops.

## Sour cream glasses

These charming tumblers were once free gifts with purchase. Companies began selling food in keepsake glassware in the 1920s, but the concept really took off after World War II, when Penn Maid and Breakstone offered sour cream in these colorful vessels with pry-off lids. The graphics evolved from wheat and diamonds in the 1950s to daisies (shown here) and regional themes in the 1960s and '70s. Search them out online or at thrift stores.

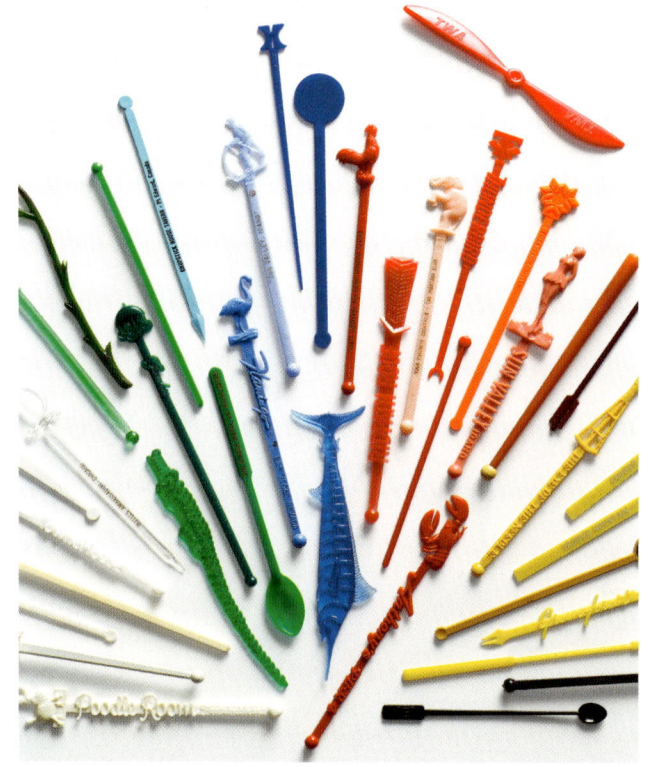

## Champagne coupes

While Europeans have long favored flutes, which admittedly preserve the bubbles longer than coupes, manufacturing companies in the Ohio River Valley, such as Cambridge Glass and Duncan & Miller, shifted production in the early twentieth century to suit Americans' taste for the shallower, showier glass style. Some have colored stems or bases, and many feature intricate wheel-cut engraving. Due to their delicate nature, a complete vintage set is rare, but individual glasses can be found for as little as five dollars, and a collection of mismatched ones creates a sophisticated, eclectic look.

# Engraved Crystal

Featuring fine-cut depictions of everything from flora and fauna to heavenly objects, engraved crystal glassware—as well as vases, plates, compotes, and decanters—are a collector's dream, serving practical purposes for entertaining and decorating.

## Secrets to Success

### ▶ AVAILABILITY

Despite their fragility, many engraved tumblers, cordial glasses, wine glasses, and Champagne flutes from the eighteenth to early twentieth centuries have survived. Large quantities of vintage crystal can typically be found in antiques stores and at auctions, suitable for use or display as decorative objects.

### ▶ METHOD

These engravings were produced for centuries by skilled craftsmen using copper or stone wheels lubricated with sand and oil. The wheel was rotated by a foot treadle, allowing freehand creation of shaded patterns, graphic designs, or detailed botanical motifs.

### ▶ ORIGIN

Key production centers in the eighteenth and nineteenth centuries included Bohemia and Ireland; nineteenth-century American Ohio Valley glass is also valued. Designs were widely copied, making origin identification difficult. Focus on quality of artistry and workmanship; some later pieces have maker signatures on the base.

### ▶ SAFETY

True crystal contains lead oxide (varying by region), giving it greater brilliance, weight, and a clear ring when tapped, compared to ordinary glass. It is softer, making it easier to engrave. Lead content is generally safe for normal use, provided acidic liquids are not stored in it for extended periods.

# 3

# GROUP LIKE ITEMS TOGETHER

Displaying collectibles en masse is generally more striking than when they are spread throughout the home or tucked away for safekeeping. To keep them from appearing cluttered, the key is to organize the pieces for a curated, cohesive look. You can achieve this with a unified display method that establishes visual order and showcases the items for maximum impact.

**Sort items by a shared trait or theme.** Unify your collection by grouping pieces with a shared characteristic, such as color, pattern, material, or shape. For example, an arrangement of all-white ceramics will create a harmonious display, as will a wall display of patterned plates in various shades of the same hue. I display my own collection of yellowware bowls (opposite) on deep shelves lining the hallway between the kitchen and library. When arranging a multihued collection, such as bold midcentury kitchen enamelware on mounted shelves, consider repeating smaller groupings of the same color throughout.

**Add visual interest.** On a shelf or table, arrange items of different heights, profiles, and sizes; you can also use pedestals or other risers to elevate smaller pieces. For a china cabinet or plate rack arrangement, mix up the pieces, with platters and plates resting upright in the background and cups and other smaller pieces standing before them.

**Apply the rule of odds.** An odd number of items (three, five, seven, and so on) is often more pleasing to the eye than even-numbered groupings, making it feel more dynamic and less static.

**Corral smaller items.** Group individual collectibles on a large tray so they read as a single unit, or display tiny ones (such as shells, buttons, wooden eggs, or pretty rocks) in an attractive glass jar or other clear vessel.

**Think vertically.** If space is limited, try stacking bulky items like vintage suitcases in a corner (or folded quilts on a spare chair) to turn them into an artful arrangement. You can also display throws or blankets on a rustic ladder, or frame certain collectibles (such as infant apparel or fabric samples) for a gallery wall.

**Create vignettes.** Instead of isolating your collection, incorporate it into your home's décor, such as by arranging the items alongside books or houseplants.

**Rotate pieces regularly.** If you have more items than can be displayed tastefully, store the extras in labeled bins (see page 196) and swap the items seasonally or annually to keep your display feeling fresh.

This studied vignette features a unique lidded Wedgwood Louise tureen, a rectangular Melbourne platter by Gildea & Walker, a T&R Boote Blackberry pitcher notable for its delicate spider web, and a Rangoon gravy boat by manufacturer Emery Burslem.

# Transferware

Developed in the mid-1700s in Staffordshire, England, transferware is available in many different styles and designs. The bold yet intricate pieces produced during the Aesthetic Movement (1860 to 1900) are especially popular for their modern-day appeal. Heed these tips for assembling your own collection.

## Secrets to Success

▸ **UNDERSTAND ITS ORIGINS.**
Transferware may be synonymous with the Victorian era, but the technique predates Queen Victoria herself. Developed in the mid-eighteenth century, transfer printing allowed intricate designs—engraved on copper plates, transferred to paper, and pressed onto earthenware—to be reproduced quickly.

▸ **LEARN TO RECOGNIZE THE EARLY LOOK.**
Before the Aesthetic Movement, transferware closely mimicked hand-painted ceramics. Look for borders that resemble delicate bobbin lace, embellished with flowers, ribbons, and medallions. At the center is often a detailed scene—foreign landscapes, romantic vignettes, exotic animals, or historical figures such as Napoleon and Wellington.

▸ **APPRECIATE THE IMPORTANCE OF FORM.**
Victorian transferware is as much about shape as surface. Plates and platters often feature scalloped edges, teapots are generously curved, and handles twist and curl with flourish.

▸ **RECOGNIZE WHEN TASTES SHIFTED.**
By the mid-nineteenth century, collectors and consumers alike began to tire of familiar patterns. Transferware's durability meant pieces didn't need frequent replacing, so British andn American potteries adapted.

▸ **EMBRACE VARIETY AND CROSSCURRENTS.**
Later transferware draws inspiration from everywhere: Persian ogees, classical cities, Arts and Crafts flowers, English chintz, and Japanese sparrows all appear, alongside children, domestic animals, and zoological creatures. The results can feel quirky, rich with cultural influences layered together.

▸ **LOOK FOR AESTHETIC MOVEMENT CUES.**
During the Aesthetic Movement, many transferware designers abandoned the idea of a plate as a framed picture. Instead, they treated the surface as a canvas to be fully covered. Shapes grew simpler and more geometric. And like the art of its time, Aesthetic Movement transferware grew increasingly abstract and, unlike the pastoral scenes and historical sites depicted on other transferware, borrowed heavily from Japanese art and culture.

▸ **KNOW THE MATERIALS AND MARKETS.**
Brown-and-white ironstone pieces were produced for less affluent buyers and remain among the most accessible for collectors today. Multicolored examples are more expensive, since each color required a separate firing. At the high end, manufacturers such as Minton and Copeland used fine porcelain, steel-cut engravings, touches of gold, and overpainting or lustre.

▸ **COLLECT WITH CONFIDENCE—AND USE YOUR PIECES.**
Because so much transferware was made in England and the United States, good examples are easy to find at flea markets and antiques shops. Brown-and-white plates are often quite affordable, with polychrome pieces commanding higher prices. Transferware is durable for everyday use—just avoid the dishwasher. Hanging plates on a wall, arranging them in a cupboard, or setting a table with many patterns creates a look that is unmistakably inviting.

THIS PAGE: A mix of classical styles rest harmoniously on open shelving. OPPOSITE PAGE: Japanese-influenced Aesthetic Movement designs blend beautifully with Arts and Crafts pieces and Wedgwood's popular Marigold pattern. The floral-patterned salad servers are my own.

Embodying age-old craftsmanship, each of these pieces reflects the care of its maker—whether handblown glass produced in Scandinavia or lunch boxes and glazed animal planters from Ohio—and brings a touch of artistry to everyday life.

## Stoneware crocks

The ultradurable vessels, plentiful in antiques shops, were first produced in England in the mid-1800s and soon lined general-store shelves across America and Europe, containing preserved food and drink. High-temperature firing lent some a toasted finish (center) and extra protection from acidic or briny goods, such as pickles. Fill yours with kitchen tools or fall branches, or display one of these sculptural beauties on their own. Their shapes hint at what was once stored inside: Former liquor bottles (second from right) are tall and slender, with necks for cork stoppers, while marmalade jars (far right) are wide and fluted for an easy grip.

⌄

## Bubble bud vases

After the Second World War, Swedish, Danish, and Czech glassmakers started producing a new kind of handblown bud vase. Each is intended to hold a single stem and then be clustered with others. The round, weighty bases that distinguish them look sculptural but also serve a practical purpose: anchoring a heavy bloom. And since they are affordable finds, you can buy a handful to artfully group on a table or along a windowsill.

## Celery glasses

Celery may strike you more as a staple of a crudités platter than an edible centerpiece. But back in the early nineteenth century, the leafy vegetable was such a delicacy and status symbol that a formal vessel was made just to serve it. Today, clear pressed-glass versions from Pittsburgh, a city once known for its glassworks industry, are not hard to find. Blown-glass vases from the UK (second from right), with their intricately cut details and popular motifs, such as the lion's-head stem (front center), are highly coveted by collectors.

## Animal-shaped ceramics

These adorable glazed animal planters—perfectly sized for a single cactus or jade plant—hail from a variety of makers, but many were produced between the 1930s and the '50s in the small town of Roseville, Ohio, which was then famous for its ceramics. Their playful forms and painterly hues make even well-loved examples highly sought-after by collectors. Ones with their original hand-painted face, like the frog at lower left by McCoy, are also especially desirable. Simply clear off a sunny ledge to give your menagerie a charming place to perch. They would look particularly fetching arranged on shelves in a nursery or kids' room and just might spark a collecting interest in the next generation.

⌄

## Lunch boxes

By the 1930s, schoolchildren had begun carrying their lunches in sturdy metal pails, trading brown paper bags for reusable containers that were both practical and decorative. Production slowed during World War II, when metal was diverted for the war effort. Soon thereafter, lunch pails returned in a cheerful array of patterns, themes, and graphics. Ohio Art favored oval-shaped tins adorned with trains and sports pennants, while Aladdin outfitted its iconic box with a fitted compartment for a thermos (as in the red plaid design, center). Today, these nostalgic containers are easy to spot at flea markets and tag sales. Look for one in good condition, and repurpose it to hold an afternoon snack, corral art supplies, or bring order to a desk drawer.

# Pincushions

Until the mid-nineteenth century, quality pins were expensive to produce. Victorian-era pincushions were similarly fancy, made from silk or velvet with intricate beading as well as silver. Once mechanization made pins plentiful, larger-scale commercial production of pincushions took off. The tomato (with a dangling emery-filled strawberry, for sharpening needles) is the easiest vintage one to find. Other motifs include oranges (top, with white strip), many of which hide a retractable tape measure in the stem; geometric puzzle balls (upper left) take a cue from quilting patterns. Stash them in a sewing basket or on view in large glass jars.

# 4

# PROTECT YOUR COLLECTIONS

Rather than hide collections away, store or display them so you can readily employ and enjoy your finds, preferably where you will use them. Examples include copper pots and pans on a hanging rack near the range, cookie cutters tucked inside a drawer for baking sessions, and decanters on a bar cart or a sideboard for at-the-ready entertaining. Of course, more sizable collections may require long-term storage where you rotate the items, in which case you'll want to heed the following guidance.

**Provide optimal environmental conditions.** Choose a cool, dry location with stable temperatures (around 70°F and 50 percent humidity) to prevent damage from heat, mold, and degradation.

**Protect against fading.** Keep collections away from direct sunlight and bright artificial lights (this also applies when displaying items not in storage).

**Prevent warping.** Stack records and books vertically, and always avoid stacking heavy items on top of delicate ones.

**Use the right materials.** Store collectibles in acid-free, archival-quality storage containers, such as plastic sleeves, bags, bins, and boxes, and cushion fragile items with soft, nonabrasive materials like crumpled tissue paper, newsprint, or batting. Be sure to wrap items individually so they don't come into contact with one another.

**Label everything.** Mark all storage containers with their contents for easy identification and to minimize handling.

▸ **MARTHA COLLECTS**
I first met the late David Rockefeller, a son of John D. Rockefeller, Jr., in 1997, shortly after I purchased Skylands in Seal Harbor, Maine. He was the first of my new neighbors to call—and soon invited me to dinner, introducing me to the "Rockefeller" style of entertaining. The food was always delicious, but what I remember most is the tableware. David took immense pleasure in setting a table, whether at his contemporary home in Maine, his farm in Pocantico Hills, surrounded by fine art, antiques, and garden flowers, or in his New York townhouse, where we dined on his beautifully hand-painted collection of china (such as the English Derby platter, opposite) that reflected his late wife Peggy's love of nature. Those gatherings left a lasting impression on me, as did David himself—his warmth, his friendship, and his deep appreciation for fine food and gracious dining.

# Copper Kitchenware

One of my favorite collections is my trove of copper cookware and bakeware, which includes antique English, French, and American pieces amassed over the years. Copper is rustic, elegant, utilitarian, and decorative. I always buy shapes that I like.

## Secrets to Success

▸ **BEGIN WITH CURIOSITY AND RESEARCH.**
I bought my first copper cookware in Paris in 1961, shortly after reading *Mastering the Art of French Cooking* from cover to cover, and was eager to take the advice of Julia Child, Louisette Bertholle, and Simone Beck when it came to assembling my supply of kitchenware. "Copper pots are the most satisfactory of all to cook in," the groundbreaking authors wrote.

▸ **START WITH ONE INDISPENSABLE PIECE.**
Everyone should have at least one piece. Indeed, the metal is an excellent heat conductor, which allows for better control and precision. I began with saucepans, which I bought from E. Dehillerin, the venerable kitchen-supply store in Paris, and then added sauté pans and stockpots. You don't need an entire set at once.

▸ **COLLECT WITH AN EYE TOWARD HISTORY.**
European cooks have appreciated copper's fine qualities for centuries. Stately home and restaurant kitchens in the mid-nineteenth century were stocked with copper cookware, as well as intricate and fanciful molds for ice creams, mousses, and jellies. When you buy one of these early pieces, you're owing a piece of culinary history.

▸ **BE OPEN TO UNEXPECTED FINDS.**
I haven't sought out only the rarest of the rare. Over the years, I've also picked up many twentieth-century pieces, their luster dulled by tarnish, from tag sales and consignment shops. Many people no longer wanted to polish it, which made these pieces surprisingly affordable.

▸ **USE COPPER AS BOTH TOOL AND ORNAMENT.**
When I updated the kitchen at the Maple House, a 1970s ranchlike home on the northernmost part of my Bedford property, I decided to create striking displays for my ever-growing collection, which I brought over from the kitchen in my main Bedford house (and my kitchen at Turkey Hill, in Westport, Connecticut, before that). It's all so beautiful to look at and easy to use, and the copper casts a warm glow over the entire room. Here are my display tips:

- ☐ Open shelving, in both the island and floor-to-ceiling cabinetry, showcases the items and allows easy access; the copper pops against the painted-black background.

- ☐ A copper ceiling rack near the stoves keeps the pots and pans within arm's reach.

- ☐ An antique oak plate rack, pulled out of storage, fits nicely above one of the two sinks and holds antique copper dishes.

- ☐ Pride of place on the stovetop goes to the copper kettle used to boil water for my daily green tea.

▸ **LET THE COLLECTION EVOLVE NATURALLY.**
My copper has followed me from kitchen to kitchen over the years, growing slowly and thoughtfully.

THIS PAGE: I have a collection of ale pitchers in various sizes; they were used in English pubs during the 1920s and '30s. OPPOSITE PAGE: I make molded ice creams in these rare nineteenth-century molds, each more than a foot tall and featuring a dramatic swag design.

A collection of English and French copper molds, with some 1950s hardware-store models mixed in, showcase brilliantly against the clean lines of this Danish rosewood furniture.

# 5

# EVOLVE YOUR COLLECTIONS

Collecting is a lifelong pursuit and a way to connect your past, present, and future. Growing your assortment also keeps the collection—and your life—more interesting, as you can be on the lookout for new finds when traveling or visiting antiques shops. Like all passionate collectors, you will soon find yourself scanning the environment for the things you collect, without thinking.

**Trust your instincts.** If a piece evokes an emotional response, it is a meaningful addition. Don't overthink it (unless cost is an issue; then it's worth the extra assessment).

**Mix high and low.** Not all collectibles need to be expensive or rare. Combine pricier, one-of-a-kind items with bargain finds from flea markets, thrift stores, or estate sales. This mix will reflect a more organic approach and will enable you to add pieces affordably.

**Leverage online resources.** Websites like Etsy, eBay, 1stdibs, and even Facebook Marketplace are great for finding specific pieces and comparing prices.

**Forge a network.** Establish relationships with antiques dealers and companies that handle estate sales and auctions, both locally and nationwide (depending on your collection). Follow them on social media and sign up for email notifications. You can also join online forums to connect with fellow enthusiasts.

**Attend the major fairs**. Make a point of visiting multivendor events for a truly one-stop shopping extravaganza (and to meet people who deal in your target collectibles). Brimfield (Massachusetts) and Round Top (Texas) are the largest such antiques events, each taking place three times per year—not to mention one of Europe's biggest flea markets, the Paris Flea Market (Marché aux Puces de Saint-Ouen). But those are just the most well-known (and widely attended); search for markets in your direct area or any place you might be visiting.

**Be patient.** Once again, it's not about stockpiling as many items as possible all at once. To truly build a collection that resonates with you on a personal level takes time. It also creates anticipation and allows you to shop with intention—and to be open to serendipitous finds, like a gorgeous cake stand in an out-of-the-way shop during a weekend getaway. Slow down and enjoy the journey.

**Consider a legacy project.** There's no better reason to devote time to collecting items that you love than the sheer pleasure derived from sharing your finds with others and in passing down your prized collection to the next generation.

# ▶ BAKING COLLECTIBLES

These pieces reflect a time when baking was both craft and ceremony. Displayed or put back to use, they remind us that beauty has always had a place alongside utility—and that the joy of baking begins long before the oven is turned on.

## Ceramic pie birds

Reminiscent of the line "Four and twenty blackbirds baked in a pie" from the Mother Goose nursery rhyme, these ceramic pie birds are not just charming adornments. The creatures, popularized in 1700s England, also serve a practical purpose—specifically, they allow steam to escape from (mostly savory) pies during baking. Today, the flea-market finds are beloved collectibles and remain interesting because they made a novelty out of a household task and are sturdy enough to be used for their intended purpose. Between uses, display them on a kitchen shelf for a sweet vignette. The most common variety—black with a yellow beak—sell for as little as a dollar each; more colorful birds or other animals generally cost more.

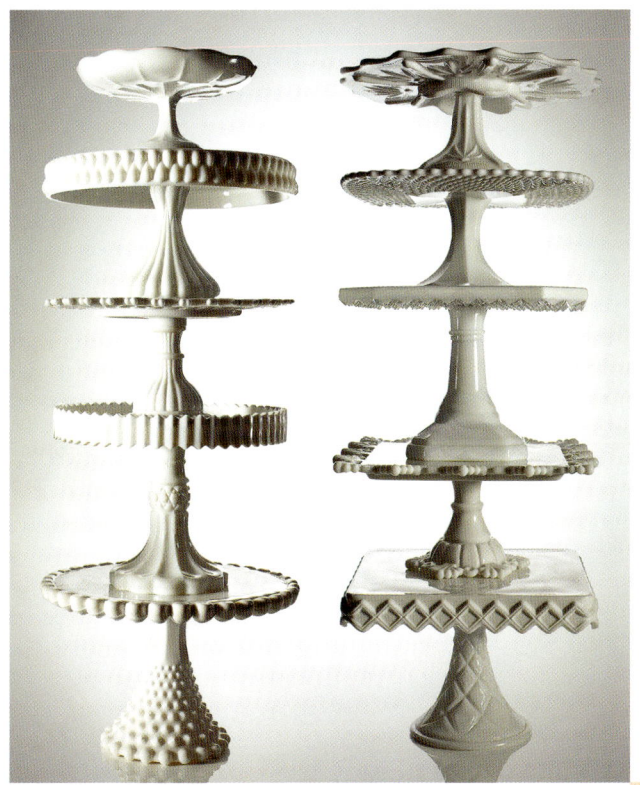

## Cookie cutters

Vintage or new, these charming tools have been shaping sweet memories for decades. The earliest shown here (such as the heart with the round hole in its back, center) date to the nineteenth century. Mass-produced tin cutters came next, followed by aluminum cutters—common in the 1930s—and then plastic cutters a decade later. Copper became popular and collectible later in the twentieth century. Designs with flat backs and holes generally predated those with handles. But it's difficult to date a cutter definitively, because so many reproductions have been made and tin ages quickly, looking well worn even when it's not. In addition to heart cutters, ideal for Valentine's Day, cutters come in practically every shape imaginable, so pick those that appeal to you the most, or collect a wide variety to cover all your baking pursuits.

## Cake stands

Most cake stands were produced between 1850 and 1950. The largest versions (once used in window displays of bake shops) are rare and often more expensive, as are colored stands. Vibrant shades didn't crop up until the 1870s, when eye-catching hues grew trendy in home décor, and the demand for colored glassware followed. A stand of pretty blue or green also looked good next to exotic fruits, which became more available with the advent of train travel. White pressed milk glass came into vogue in the 1880s. When it returned in the 1950s, the era of the pink-tiled bathroom, it also came in pink. If you find a stand you'd like to buy, check the crispness of the design, an important detail for collectors. Molds wore down with use, and the later a stand was made from one, the less sharp and sparkly it would be. But some scratches are normal and expected. After all, the stands were made to be used for celebrations.

# GARDENING

Gardening is, for me, more than a pastime. It is a way of life. My earliest lessons came when I was growing up, when composting kitchen scraps, tending the soil, and harvesting vegetables with my father were simply daily activities. Those habits stayed with me and deepened years later at Turkey Hill in Westport, Connecticut, where I designed and maintained a sizable vegetable garden to supply my catering business. Growing my own produce wasn't just economical—it ensured quality, variety, and flavor you could never count on elsewhere. From the beginning, gardening taught me that success depends on careful preparation, keen observation, and steady nurturing.

When I moved to my farm in Bedford, New York, I deliberately decided to rethink the way I had always gardened, using the property as a proving ground for new ideas. With far more land than my Turkey Hill garden—and a landscape that seemed to absorb plants at an astonishing rate—I shifted from the richly layered borders and continuous color inspired by Monet and Helena Rutherfurd Ely to a philosophy rooted in mass, restraint, and sequence. Influenced by designers and writers such as Jacques Wirtz and Elizabeth von Arnim, I began working in terms of areas rather than individual beds, allowing distinct plantings to take turns commanding attention across the landscape. A large peony garden, designed as a single, focused gesture of color, is one example of this approach and of how the Bedford property continues to teach me new lessons.

That same evolution deepened my long-standing love affair with trees, which began at Turkey Hill, where I first understood their power to lend beauty, structure, and meaning to a residential landscape. Even now, after thousands of trees have been planted and countless lessons learned, the work remains ongoing—and keeps my decades of experience in active use while constantly pushing it forward.

Because the plant world is vast, and to foster my endless curiosity, I continually seek inspiration to evolve and enhance my own landscape. I love studying great gardens and trusted books, and spending time visiting famous gardens while traveling. I always design on paper before digging, as it allows me to explore possibilities and avoid costly mistakes. To ensure I don't overlook the myriad tasks involved in maintaining a garden, I treat gardening as a scheduled practice, planning the year, making weekly lists, and checking in daily. Having the proper tools—and caring for them well—eases my efforts and improves efficiency.

Growing from seed, dividing perennials, planting bulbs in generous drifts, and tending vegetables and cutting flowers all stretch resources while expanding the garden's beauty and productivity. These principles—along with using container plants to add visual interest and nurturing houseplants for year-round vitality—form the backbone of my approach to gardening, as more comprehensively described in the bestselling *Martha Stewart's Gardening Handbook: The Essential Guide to Designing, Planting, and Growing.* With care and consistency, they create a garden that grows richer and more rewarding with every season.

# 1

# SEEK OUT INSPIRATION

Before you sketch out your garden designs, which is absolutely essential for any new plot, take the time to explore all the possibilities. The plant world is incredibly vast and varied, and even experienced gardeners relish the thrill of discovering yet more varieties or cultivars to add to their collection. Novice gardeners, in particular, will benefit from increasing their knowledge of the different types of plants (such as annuals versus perennials) and the different ways they can be utilized in the landscape (e.g., trees that provide shade, privacy, or a focal point).

**Consult gardening books.** You don't need a dedicated home library like mine to access the hundreds of available volumes depicting all manner of garden designs, complete with gorgeous photography, hand-sketched blueprints, and other detailed information to incorporate into your landscape. Public libraries are excellent resources, or you can check the selection at local bookstores and limit your purchases to those that resonate with you the most. Be mindful of your climate when doing your research—yes, you can experiment with plantings that aren't considered hardy for your growing zone, but avoid becoming too enamored of those that simply aren't practical for your area. On the other hand, you might discover uncommon species, such as Korean hybrid mums (shown opposite), which unlike regular mums are perennials that are hardy in colder climates (down to zone 4) and produce a cloud of daisy-like flowers ranging from white and pale yellow to dusty pink and coral.

**Study your surroundings.** Explore your neighborhood—it doesn't get more local than your very own street and the surrounding vicinity. Take inspiration from plants and gardens that you like. Trees, shrubs, and perennial flowers that are thriving next door or on a nearby block are likely to do so in your yard, too. And when you travel, try to visit exemplary gardens to bring fresh ideas home.

> ▸ **MARTHA GARDENS**
> I am constantly searching out gardens around the world, from the formal ones of England and other European countries to the more naturalistic examples in Japan, along with Japanese-style gardens across the US, including the Asticou Azalea Garden in Maine, the Japanese American Museum of Oregon, and the Morikami Museum and Japanese Gardens in Florida. My love of these gardens is evident at my Bedford farm, where I have incorporated traditional elements, such as allées, pergolas, and boxwood borders, along with an area devoted to hundreds of Japanese maple trees. Even if you can't travel to such places in person, you can explore them and countless others online.

**Browse a reputable local nursery.** Stroll the aisles to see which plants strike you, noting their space and light requirements to see whether and how they could fit into your designs. Ask a staff member to help you achieve specific goals, such as creating a striking shade garden or a border garden in a chosen palette, bringing any photos or sketches of the various sites. Doing this will also ensure that you buy plants known to be suitable for your zone, including annuals that will last only one season.

**Attend garden tours and shows.** By visiting a local botanical garden, you'll reap ideas and inspiration in spades, especially when they showcase native plants, which best support pollinators and other area wildlife. Gather ideas by strolling the grounds, snapping photos along the way, and check the website for dates of special "grow shows," plant sales, and hands-on workshops (always a great way to master new skills). Certain conservancies offer seasonal tours of private gardens, where you might also meet the homeowner and have an opportunity to ask questions.

> ▶ **MARTHA GARDENS**
> There are a few events that go on my calendar each year that I consider sacrosanct: my family's birthdays, my summer vacation at my house in Maine, my holiday parties, and Trade Secrets. Almost nothing can cause me to miss these. Trade Secrets is a very interesting rare plant and garden antiques sale that is held each year in Connecticut. It attracts thousands of shoppers every spring and benefits a very worthy local group, Women's Support Services. Established in 2000 by interior designer Bunny Williams, Trade Secrets brings together in one place for one day more than 60 growers, antiques dealers, artisans, and plantsmen and -women who specialize in the rare, the special, the unusual, and the coveted. It is the one place where, if you get there early and stay late, you can visit with suppliers from all over the Northeast. Because I garden most weekends in spring and summer and work on weekdays, I would find it almost impossible to go to each exhibitor's greenhouse or shop to find what I can locate here in one day.
>
> Many of the buyers make a weekend of this special event, shopping at Trade Secrets and touring the wonderful celebrated local gardens. I generally have so many plants that I need to spend a full day planting them. But I can promise that should you attend, you will not be disappointed in the quality of the lovely gardens on the tour, you will learn a tremendous amount about the plant material that thrives in this special corner of our country, and you will be able to converse with some of our finest gardening experts. You will also be benefiting a good cause.

# Essential Gardening Tools

**Similar to cooking supplies, the proper gardening implements can greatly enhance your efficiency and productivity. Whether you're an avid gardener or just getting started, reliable tools will help you tackle both big and small gardening tasks, year in and year out.**

| Tools | What to Look For |
|-------|------------------|
| ▶ **GLOVES** | Get a good pair of gardening gloves with a nonslip grip to allow you to safely perform myriad tasks and keep your hands clean when weeding, digging, and more. Wash them as needed to prevent soil buildup, and let air-dry in the sun (for antimicrobial purposes). |
| ▶ **SECATEURS** | Test out different secateurs—also known as pruning shears—as these should effortlessly cut through branches, shrubs, fruit trees, creepers, and more. Find a model that is sharp, easy to use, and has covered handles so that your hands don't slip, along with a safety clip to secure the blade when not in use. |
| ▶ **TROWEL** | This handheld shovel comes in different sizes: An all-purpose trowel has a 6- to 8-inch blade, while a short, narrow trowel is helpful for tight spaces and container plants; a wider, longer trowel is for digging holes and lifting heavier plants. Some trowels are designed with depth markings for precise planting. Scoop-shaped trowels are useful for potting and moving soil, while others feature a pointed blade for digging in rugged or rocky soil. |
| ▶ **HORI HORI** | This ancient Japanese gardening tool features a serrated edge and is prized for its versatility in weeding, digging, dividing, and cutting through leaves and stems. Models with measurements on the blade let you know how deep you are digging. |
| ▶ **T-HANDLED DIBBER** | This specialty tool works by manually pressing the sharp tip into the soil to make appropriate holes for planting bulbs. It should have a durable steel shaft that is seamlessly connected to an easy-to-grip wooden handle featuring depth markings. |
| ▶ **SHOVEL AND SPADE** | As genuine workhorses, these tools should feel solid and well balanced in your hands, with a forged steel blade (rounded for shovels, flat for spades) and durable ash wood handles. |
| ▶ **RAKES** | Ideally, get two rakes—a regular one for gathering leaves and debris, and a bed preparation rake (with rigid tines and a wide, flat head) for leveling planting beds, breaking up clods, spreading soil or compost evenly, and preparing the ground before planting. |
| ▶ **PLANT MARKERS** | Use these identifiers to label plant names and keep track of where everything is planted. You can buy markers made of wood, galvanized tin, or other all-weather materials at nurseries; or employ Popsicle sticks or other household supplies. |
| ▶ **GARDEN TWINE** | Use this indispensable tool to mark out straight rows and beds, tie up stakes and structures (like bamboo tepees for tomatoes or trellises for climbing vines), and secure burlap covers around outdoor planters in winter. |

# 2
# SCHEDULE IN GARDENING

Of all the routines of daily life, gardening is the one most likely to get out of hand if left to chance. There are simply too many time-sensitive steps and repeat tasks to commit to memory—especially during the summer, when so many other activities compete for your attention. Plus, depending on where you live, the growing season can be rather short, making it all the more imperative for you to stay on top of the garden rather than vice versa. Adopting my sensible organizing tips and tools will help not only in the current season but in years to come.

**Add routine garden tasks to your annual calendar.** Do this at the start of each year. These range from ordering seeds and supplies in January, checking gardening tools in March, testing and remediating the soil in April, planting spring bulbs in October, and bringing all the container plants inside before the expected date of the first frost (ask your local garden center or cooperative extension).

**Make weekly to-do lists.** To ensure that everything is ready for the growing season, begin your list-making in March (or earlier, depending on where you live) and continue right through fall. This consistent habit will help you stay on top of all the different tasks across the gardening season, so nothing is overlooked.

**Check on your garden daily.** Establish a regular habit of visiting your garden first thing in the morning or after work, whichever best suits your schedule. This ensures you can tackle tasks and any issues right away and do a little bit each day, so the weeding, watering, and pruning feel a lot less overwhelming.

> ▸ **MARTHA GARDENS**
> I make a gardening plan for the coming week every Sunday evening, with the listed tasks dependent upon the time of year. And each day that I am home, I am in the garden by 7 A.M., just after finishing Pilates, for a daily check-in.

**Monitor your garden's progress.** To help keep track of changes from year to year, document what blooms when—either in your garden journal or with photos (or both). And once or twice a month, you can track what you've planted, what's doing well, and what you want to grow in the future to help you form a plan for the next year—for example, choosing plants for a meandering gravel pathway.

# 3

# SET UP A HOME COMPOSTING SYSTEM

Crumbly, dark-brown finished compost is by far the most effective and versatile way to enrich your garden's soil to help it retain moisture and nutrients, thereby promoting the health and well-being of your plants. Rather than purchase it by the bag or the truckload (the more economical and efficient of the two options), you can easily produce it yourself, putting everyday kitchen scraps and yard trimmings to excellent use. Composting does take some effort to get started, but then nature will take over from there. And you will save so much money in the long run, both by not having to buy compost and by protecting the investment you've made in your plants.

> ▶ **MARTHA GARDENS**
> Composting has always been a part of my life. When I was a child, my family kept a small bucket next to the kitchen sink where all food scraps (except meat or fat) were deposited. The bucket was emptied every day onto the compost heap at the back of the yard. My dad talked with excitement about the transformation of these scraps into "black gold," a substance he said would revitalize his backyard gardens, returning nutrients to the soil. This early inspiration instilled in me a set of organic gardening practices and good habits for healthy soil and plants that I regularly employ to this very day.

**Know what cannot be composted.** Rather than memorize all that can be composted, it is easier—and more important—to remember what to avoid, as these items will not properly break down and can contaminate the final product: meat and bones; cooking fats and fatty foods (like nut butters); dairy products; paper receipts and shipping labels (which contain harmful chemicals, unlike regular paper products); plastic (even if it's labeled "compostable"); glossy or colorful cardboard; ashes from a charcoal grill; and diseased plant material.

**Follow the recommended ratio.** The general proportion is to layer one-third green, nitrogenous matter—kitchen scraps (including produce scraps and peels, egg shells, coffee grounds, and tea leaves), grass clippings, and healthy plant cuttings—and two-thirds carbon-rich brown matter, from dried leaves, pine needles, straw and hay, wood chips, and shredded cardboard and newspaper (helpful when dried yard waste is limited). Note that you can also include weeds as green matter because the compost will reach a high-enough temperature to kill their seeds.

**Choose your location.** Select a spot with good drainage to prevent sogginess and ensure proper air circulation. Partial sunlight is ideal, as too much sun can dry out the pile, while too much shade can slow decomposition. Convenience to a water source is also helpful for keeping the pile moist; proximity to your gardens will make application easier, too.

**Contain the compost.** There is no one right way to house your compost, but keeping it enclosed will prevent pets and wildlife from accessing it. The size of your composting system will depend on the amount of waste you generate and the amount of finished compost you need to nurture your garden. Having at least two bins—one that is actively decomposing, the other ready to use—is an efficient setup. Containers designed for composting are available in various sizes at home improvement stores and online. When possible, opt for plastic-free options, such as those made from breathable mesh. Some people even construct four-sided enclosures with wooden pallets set on their sides.

**Start the pile.** Begin with a base layer of twigs or mulch for aeration and drainage. Next, layer brown and green materials, aiming for the 2:1 ratio of browns to greens. Chop up everything as it is added to expedite decomposition. Continue layering until you have a pile at least 3 feet deep, adding a thin layer of garden soil in the middle of the pile to promote microorganisms and ending with a layer of brown materials.

**Turn the pile.** After a week, you'll notice the pile heat up. Turn it with a pitchfork, mixing the layers. As the pile continues to "cook" and reduce, turn it every few days, and keep adding more layers, ending with brown. (If your compost seems like it isn't doing anything, you may need to add more water and/or green ingredients.) Turning provides oxygen for the microorganisms and facilitates rapid, even decomposition. The more frequently you turn the compost, the sooner it will be ready.

**Monitor moisture levels.** The compost pile should consistently feel like a wrung-out sponge, so add water as needed. Additionally, adjust the ratio of browns to greens if the pile becomes too wet or too dry, respectively.

**Harvest your compost.** It's ready when it has turned a brownish-black color and is free of recognizable ingredients, with no offensive odor. Depending on the ingredients and conditions, this process can take anywhere from six months to a year. You can sieve it to remove any large particles before using it in your garden.

# 4

# PREPARE YOUR SOIL

The health and quality of your soil are paramount because the soil provides plants with the vital nutrients, water, and air they need to thrive and grow strong roots, leading to a healthy and productive garden. By understanding and improving your soil through testing, adding organic matter like compost, and ensuring good drainage and aeration, you create the ideal "living ecosystem" for your plants to flourish.

**Do a soil test.** Determine the health of your soil by checking for deficiencies in nutrients and assessing its composition. Testing can also let you know the soil's pH, or acidity. Most plants prefer neutral soil (pH 6 to 7), though azaleas, rhododendrons, hollies, and other plants thrive in moderately acidic soil (pH 5 to 6). You can purchase a home testing kit from a garden center or online. Many local cooperative extension services can also perform a detailed analysis of a soil sample you provide.

**Enrich the soil.** When preparing a new garden area, be sure to mix in plenty of organic matter such as compost, manure, or high-quality mixes to create a looser, airier soil that better holds moisture and nutrients. This step will also encourage and support the growth of healthy root systems and help plants resist pests and diseases naturally. Add 3 to 6 inches of fresh organic mix to new beds as well as existing ones on a yearly basis.

> ▸ **MARTHA GARDENS**
> If you are planning on using raised beds, be sure to purchase an organic soil mix designed for that purpose, formulated to drain well while still retaining moisture, usually combining compost, topsoil, and aerating materials. It also feeds plants gradually, and creates the ideal environment for strong root systems and consistent growth.

**Amend as needed.** A loamy soil, which is a balanced mix of sand, clay, and silt, is ideal for most plants. Sandy soil tends to drain too quickly, whereas dense clay soil does not drain enough. Adding organic matter can help with both of these issues. Applying lime is a common way to raise the pH of soil; applying sulfur lowers the pH.

**Apply mulch.** Once you've made the necessary amendments, cover the soil with organic mulch, such as leaves, hay, or wood chips, to help it retain moisture, regulate the temperature, prevent weed growth, and continually enrich the soil as it decomposes.

# 5

# START SEEDS INDOORS

Starting flowers and vegetables from seed allows for a far greater variety than when buying seedlings or container-grown plants from a nursery. This method is also much more economical, especially if you have sizable gardens to fill—the average cost of a seed packet is less than four dollars and can contain dozens or more seeds. Starting the seeds indoors allows you to get a jump start on spring, timing the planting so the seedlings are ready for transplanting after the last risk of frost has passed in your area. Here's how to follow my lead.

**Order seeds early and from reliable sources.** Each December, I pore over mail-order catalogs, including Johnny's Selected Seeds, Baker Creek Heirloom Seeds, Seed Savers Exchange (ideal for heirloom tomatoes, peppers, and melons), and *The Whole Seed Catalog* (at over 500 pages, it's the most comprehensive, with gorgeous photos modeled on *The Whole Earth Catalog*).

**Create an organizing system.** Sort the seeds by plant variety and keep them in their original packets whenever possible, as they include all the essential information for planting, nurturing, and harvesting. The packets can then be stored in accordion file holders or plastic tubs with sleeves and kept in a spare refrigerator until you are ready to plant them, up to several seasons.

**Buy the supplies.** You'll need a few basics, which can be easily found at garden centers and online. These include a starter tray with multiple cells and clear plastic covers; an organic, soil-free seed-starting mix; and a waterproof heating mat and grow light (both optional).

> ▸ **MARTHA GARDENS**
> I prefer a starting mix that's one part sphagnum moss and one part vermiculite, with some perlite added for better drainage. I also like to use a hand seed sower for sowing smaller seeds, such as violas. For transplanting, I use a metal widger tool (which resembles a tiny shoehorn) that can easily scoop out the seedling while keeping the roots intact.

**Prepare the trays.** Fill the cells with moistened starting mix. Make shallow indentations using a long side of a ruler or a paint-mixing stick. This keeps the rows straight and neat. The depth depends on the type of seeds; follow the directions on the seed packet.

**Sow the seeds.** Place the individual seeds at the specified distance apart in their rows. Using the ruler or stick, carefully cover the seeds with planting material. Press the soil down lightly, such as by pressing the bottom of another cell tray over the one with the seeds.

**Germinate.** Using a watering can with a fine rose, give the trays a gentle soak, but do not overwater. Cover the seed trays with their plastic covers, and place them in a warm location, such as on a waterproof heating mat used for germination (or on top of your refrigerator). When sprouts appear, move the trays to a sunny window or under a grow light so they will become strong and green.

**Know what to look for.** Seedlings are typically ready to be transplanted when they are about 4 to 6 inches tall and have at least two sets of true leaves; the roots should also hold the shape of the cell without crumbling (test by gently lifting the seedling). This typically takes 3 to 4 weeks, although some plants may require more time.

**Harden off.** Before planting in the ground, allow the seedlings to acclimate to being outdoors for a few days by moving the trays outside for extended periods of time.

**Choose a location.** Make sure each plant will get the amount of sunlight it requires, then measure the correct spacing in the garden and plot where you will place each plant.

**Transplant.** The best time to transplant seedlings is in the morning on a cloudy day. Avoid transplanting during midday, especially on hot, sunny days. For each planting row, begin by running the handle of a shovel or rake through the soil. Gently lift a few seedlings from their cells, being careful not to tug at the stems, and lay them out evenly along the prepared rows. Use your hands to backfill the soil around the seedlings, just so they sit upright (do not plant them too deeply).

**Water.** After planting, water in gently to avoid harming the tender shoots, and continue to keep the soil moist throughout the growing season.

> ▸ **MARTHA GARDENS**
> When growing seeds indoors, I regularly thin out weak or spindly seedlings, keeping only the strongest ones (those with fleshy leaves, upright stems, and good positioning) to avoid overcrowding and stress. Some seedlings are "pricked out" and transplanted into bigger cells, pots, or flats filled with seedling mix to give the roots more room before the final outdoor planting.

# 6

# DIRECT-SOW SEEDS IN THE GROUND

This method is the most effective for the many tender plants that are susceptible to transplant shock, including peas, cucumbers, carrots, and beans (as indicated on the seed packet). It is also recommended for many annual flowers, including zinnias, sunflowers, cosmos, nasturtiums, calendula, marigolds, sweet peas, and cornflowers. Direct-sow only once the soil is workable and all risk of frost has passed.

**Prepare the soil.** Clear the area of weeds and debris, then loosen the soil with a hand cultivator or a tine rake. If planting in blocks, mark the borders with garden lime. Ensure the soil is moist but not waterlogged.

**Sow the seeds.** Follow the instructions on the seed packet for proper spacing. Broadcast sowing involves scattering seeds evenly over the bed, then lightly raking the soil to cover them. For row planting, press the handle of a rake or shovel (or a wooden stake) into the soil to use as a guide, then use your hands or a seed distributor to sow the seeds along the length of the markings as directed.

> ▶ **MARTHA GARDENS**
> I recommend a seeder rake to mark the placement of the rows. This special tool is much wider than standard rakes and has shorter tines, with plastic sleeves that you fit over the tines at the desired intervals. These sleeves are what make the deeper furrows in the soil. Pull the rake toward you as you mark the rows.

**Cover the seeds.** Pinch the soil closed over the seeds with your hands, following the depth guidelines on the seed packet. (You can also sweep a rake with the tines turned upward over the rows, being careful to brush the soil sideways to avoid disturbing the seeds.) Some seeds require light for germination, so be mindful of this when covering them to prevent impeding their growth. Gently pat down the soil to ensure good seed-to-soil contact, and label each planting area with the seed type.

**Care for the seeds.** Water in the seeds gently but thoroughly at planting time to trigger germination, and continue to keep the soil consistently moist but not soggy. You can add a layer of straw to deter birds from eating the seeds. Be sure to thin out seedlings according to the packet instructions.

**Practice succession planting.** Don't plant all the seeds in a packet at once—save some for repeat plantings over the season. This is true whether you are direct-sowing them into the ground or starting seedlings indoors. I sow seeds throughout the winter in the greenhouse, so they are ready for transplanting outdoors after the last risk of frost has passed.

# 7

# PLANT BULBS FOR SEASON-LONG BLOOMS

As some of the very first plants to peek through the ground at the end of a long winter, flowering bulbs—planted in the fall—are viewed as a harbinger of spring. And spring-planted bulbs, which bloom during summer and fall, signal your landscape's transition into autumn. Both types are certainly worth planting, but it's important to consider all your options before setting out on your plan. Know, too, that the word "bulb" includes true bulbs as well as tubers and rhizomes.

> ▸ **MARTHA GARDENS**
> I plant a large number of daffodil bulbs each year, so to save money, I order them in batches of 50, 100, 500, and 1,000. Bulbs need to be packaged very carefully to ensure they are kept in the best condition during transport. Van Engelen, one of my very favorite sources, uses netted sacks as well as paper bags and plastic pouches, depending on the bulbs' humidity needs.

**Decide what to grow.** Early bloomers like snowdrops, crocuses, daffodils, hyacinths, squills, bluebells, and tulips are some of the most common fall-planted bulbs. These bring color and texture to the garden before most other perennials and shrubs begin to leaf out or bloom, providing a wonderful shift from winter. Popular spring-planted bulbs include lilies, gladiolus, dahlias, calla lilies, agapanthus, and begonias. These will carry the lushness right through the growing season.

**Buy quality bulbs.** A high-quality bulb will be firm to the touch and relatively heavy for its size. Avoid any with soft spots or signs of mold or discoloration. Also, look at the size of the bulbs—the larger they are, the greater their potential to produce more and better-looking flowers. All bulbs should be stored in a cool, dry, dark place until planted.

**Time the planting right.** Spring bulbs should be planted in the fall a few weeks before the first frost is expected, to give them time to put down roots before the ground freezes in winter. Summer-blooming bulbs can be planted in spring after the last risk of frost has passed. Ultimately, the zone you live in will dictate the proper timing, so check with a local nursery or gardening club for guidance.

**Prepare the location.** Bulbs have different sunlight requirements, as noted on the plant label. Remove all weeds and grass from the area, and loosen the soil with a gardening fork, working 10 to 12 inches deep. Sprinkle a natural and organic fertilizer recommended explicitly for all bulbs, including daffodils, crocuses, hyacinths, and tulips, over the area. Additionally, add bone meal fertilizer to increase the phosphorus in the garden, which is essential for plants to flower.

**Plot your design.** Plant the bulbs en masse to replicate nature. You can produce an impressive show with just a few dozen, especially when planting in drifts or alongside existing plantings. The key is to group a minimum of three to five bulbs in a single hole, and to space the holes between 4 and 6 inches apart, giving them enough room to grow and multiply without competing for sunlight, water, and nutrients. Group the bulbs into different varieties, shapes, sizes, and blooming times. This will provide a more impactful display and ensure a longer splash of color through the season.

**Follow general planting guidelines.** All bulbs should be planted two to three times as deep as the bulbs are tall. For example, most daffodils will be planted 6 to 8 inches below the soil surface. First, make all the holes to track their locations and varieties easily, using a bulb trowel or a cordless drill with an augur. Always plant bulbs with the pointed end facing up. Upside-down bulbs will still grow, but it will likely take longer for the shoots to appear.

> **▶ MARTHA GARDENS**
> For larger plantings, use a no-dig method: Look for a natural depression or hollow on your property where you can place the bulbs 8 inches below ground level. Or in smaller flower beds, you can remove the top layer of soil to the proper planting depth. Scatter bulb fertilizer or amendments such as bone meal over the area and work in. First mark the plan directly on the soil surface with granular lime.

**Assess the plantings.** Take photos of the flowers in bloom so you can see what areas need filling in with more bulbs in the next fall or spring planting windows.

**Prepare for next season.** Once the flowers are spent, leave the foliage intact so it can store energy for next season's blooms. You can tie them into neat bundles until the stems turn brown, and then cut them back to the ground. After removing the foliage, apply a balanced fertilizer over the area and cover with a layer of mulch. Feed again in the fall to set the bulbs up for a successful spring reemergence.

# 8

# WATER, WEED, AND FEED

If you were to master just one lesson in this chapter, it would be the importance of watering, weeding, and fertilizing. It is impossible to overemphasize how vital these ongoing tasks are to both the short- and long-term success of your garden. Simply put, you cannot expect plants—even the most vigorous growers—to take root and thrive without your ongoing attention: You eat and drink; your plants need to eat and drink, too.

**Understand watering basics.** Watering comes first, both in importance and chronological order. It is a critical part of planting, triggering seeds to swell and sprout, and encouraging transplants (whether container-grown plants from a nursery or your own indoor seedlings) to settle into their new environment. But watering doesn't stop there, which is where many gardeners go wrong.

**Water at the right time.** Early morning is best, as the cooler temperatures allow the soil and plants to absorb more water and help prepare them to withstand the strong midday sun. Watering midday is inefficient because the moisture evaporates in the heat and can cause undue stress to plants. While a better option than afternoon watering, the evening, with its moist, cooler conditions, can create a breeding ground for diseases and pests.

**Water the right way.** Direct the water at the roots, which will take up the water and hydrate the entire plant. Spraying the foliage only leads to potential leaf damage from fungal disease; wet foliage is also prone to getting scorched by the sun. A soaker hose and a drip irrigation system are the most efficient methods for minimizing evaporation, or you can use a regular hose (without a nozzle or using the soaker function) to water individual plants around the base.

**Give plants enough water.** Many variables determine the amount of water needed. However, there are some general guidelines to follow. Periodic deep watering—where the water reaches the area 6 to 12 inches below the soil surface—is far better at promoting the development of vigorous roots than frequent shallow dousings. This equates to about 1 inch of rainfall and can take anywhere from 30 to 60 minutes of irrigation at a slow, steady stream. Newly planted trees and shrubs require extra watering to encourage root development. Give them a thorough soaking two or three times weekly during the first month and then once weekly for the rest of the first growing season. Established trees and shrubs need only biweekly watering during dry periods.

**Gauge the soil moisture.** An easy way to test the soil's water content is by probing a few inches below the surface with a wooden dowel or chopstick; moist soil will cling to the stick. If it doesn't, it's time to water. Using a rain gauge, sold at garden supply centers and online, will also help you monitor how much additional water your plants may need.

**Take steps to retain moisture.** When planting, mound up the soil around the drip line of the plant and create a trench all the way around it to catch rainfall and irrigation water. You will likely need to remake the trench after heavy rainfalls. For new and existing plants, apply a 2- to 3-inch layer of mulch on the soil surface, keeping it at least 3 inches from the trunk or base of trees and shrubs. (It's fine to have the mulch close to other plants.) Working compost into new and existing garden beds and rows will improve the soil's ability to hold water. Many gardeners will add a 1- to 2-inch layer of compost around established plants (called side- or top-dressing) before covering with a layer of mulch.

**Be diligent about weeding.** Weeds in the garden are inevitable. Left alone, so many of them quickly overtake healthy plants, stealing their sunlight, water, and soil nutrients. Consistent weeding keeps things manageable. Pulling them by hand, roots and all, is easiest after rain when the soil is loose. To help deter weeds in the first place, plant densely (as shown opposite) or layer your garden beds with mulch, as described in the previous step.

> **▶ MARTHA GARDENS**
> There are many types of tools that help with weeding. I prefer the short-handled tools best so as not to disturb any of the neighboring nonweed specimens. One of my favorites is my Japanese hand hoe, but both long- and short-handled garden hoes are ideal for chopping, weeding, and clearing garden growth. I also like to use long-handled, four-tine cultivators for breaking up soil and weeding between plantings in the garden.

**Understand feeding basics.** Fertilizer is an essential part of gardening. It boosts plant growth, improves yields, adds key nutrients to the soil, and enhances disease resistance. But applying the wrong type or amount of fertilizer or doing so at the wrong time can cause leaf burn, decreased flower production, and other issues. Furthermore, plants that are starved for essential nutrients may be more prone to environmental stresses, pest pressures, and diseases.

**Buy the right fertilizer.** There is no one-size-fits-all approach when it comes to fertilizer. Different plants have different nutritional needs. An all-purpose fertilizer has a balanced ratio of nitrogen, phosphorus, and potassium (the NPK ratio), as indicated on the package. But there are fertilizers formulated for specific plants, including those that thrive in acidic conditions, such as azaleas and gardenias, as well as options for holly and evergreens, bulbs, and vegetable crops. Slow-release granular products have a more gradual, long-lasting effect, while liquid fertilizers can be used for a quick boost. Always follow the rates listed on the packaging.

**Follow feeding schedules.** As a general rule, fertilize plants in mid-spring to help spur new growth after a harsh winter, or in summer to help refill the nutritional needs of your plants. Avoid applying fertilizers too late in the year, as the new growth would be vulnerable to cold weather. Similarly, using it too early in the spring can cause new growth to emerge before an untimely late frost.

**Apply fertilizer to wet soil.** Dry soil makes it difficult for the nutrients in fertilizer to reach your plants. Watering the soil before or after application can address this concern.

# 9

# DIVIDE PLANTS TO MULTIPLY THEIR NUMBERS

Regularly divide well-grown perennials to quickly increase the stock of multistemmed flowers, ornamental grasses, and bulbs. This form of propagation offers instant gratification: In a matter of minutes, one plant becomes two or even more, depending on the size of the original. Dividing herbaceous perennials every 3 to 5 years can also keep rapidly spreading plants under control and rejuvenate older plants.

**Choose the optimum time.** It's best to divide fall bloomers and ornamental grasses in spring. Divide spring- and summer-blooming perennials in fall. (Some tough perennials, such as hostas and daylilies, can be divided anytime.) Work in the morning, preferably when the skies are overcast.

**Prepare the plant.** A day or two before removing the plant from its existing bed, prune any fragile stems and foliage down to 6 inches from the ground, then water the plant thoroughly close to the soil surface to keep roots and soil together.

**Prepare the new planting site.** Follow the instructions on page 224 for preparing the location where the division will be transplanted, loosening the soil and enriching it with organic matter. Ensure the site matches the plant's needs in terms of suitable sunlight and moisture for long-term success.

**Dig up the plant.** Lay a tarp near the plant. Using a sharp, pointed trowel, shovel, or spading fork, dig deep on all four sides of the plant, 4 to 6 inches away from its base. Pry underneath with the tool, and gently lift out the entire clump of surrounding soil. Now dig around the entire root mass, about ¼ inch beyond the plant's outermost foliage. Go deep to avoid damaging the roots. Carefully lift the plant out onto the tarp.

**Locate the roots.** After digging it up, the majority of the roots should still be attached to the plant as a cohesive soil-and-root clump (the root ball). Healthy roots are usually firm, white or light-colored, and fibrous. Shake or gently hose off loose soil from the roots, and remove any dead leaves and stems.

**Examine the root ball.** Check the root ball to see whether there are any sections that naturally split off. Avoid pulling or tearing—handle gently. If the roots are tangled, score the sides vertically with a hori hori; also, trim any torn, bruised, or rotten roots cleanly with sharp secateurs.

**Divide the plant.** The appropriate method for division is determined by the plant's root type, as follows:

▸ Some perennials (such as hostas and heleniums) have clumping roots that are easy to separate with your hands.

▸ Others (including asters, grasses, and daylilies) will need to be pried apart using two garden forks back-to-back. If any roots refuse to snap or break neatly, don't tear them; instead, cut with secateurs.

▸ Plants with fleshy, tuberous roots (such as dahlias) will need to be sliced into sections with a hori hori or other sharp blade.

▸ Perennials with tough, massive roots or rhizomes (notably astilbe) should also be cut in two using a hori hori. Try to divide the entire root mass cleanly, in a single smooth motion. You might be able to divide the halves again to yield four substantial chunks.

**Check the division.** Make sure that every new root division has a piece of the original stem and a growth bud attached. Torn or frayed tissue heals slowly and offers an entry point for soil-borne pathogens. Discard old, woody roots from the middle of the original clump.

**Plant the divisions right away.** Dig a hole that is about twice the width of the root ball and just as deep. Set the division in the hole so the top of the root ball is even with the ground's surface. Backfill the hole with the original soil mixed with organic matter such as compost or a nutrient-rich mix, tamping it down gently to ensure good contact between the soil and the root. (If you must wait to replant, wrap the division in damp newsprint, place it in a plastic bag, seal it, and refrigerate for no longer than 2 days.)

**Nurture.** Water the new plantings (except dahlias, which should not be watered until the shoots appear) thoroughly and apply a layer of mulch to help retain moisture. Continue to water regularly for the first few months, especially if there's no rain.

> **▸ MARTHA GARDENS**
> Succulents are exceptionally good candidates for propagating—whether growing them as indoor houseplants or outdoors. No digging up and dividing is required. Instead, you can take leaf or stem cuttings from healthy specimens, allow them to dry and callus for a few days, and then place them on well-draining soil (outside) or a sterile potting mix (indoors). Avoid overwatering the propagated section—a light misting is sufficient until roots form. For houseplants, bright, indirect light and good air circulation are key. In my view, succulents thrive when you leave them alone rather than fuss over them.

# 10

# INCORPORATE CONTAINER PLANTS

Even gardeners with abundant space for both in-ground and raised beds appreciate the additional visual interest potted plants bring to the overall landscape design. Container plants can be stunning all on their own, too, in case other types of gardening are not feasible.

**Choose the plants.** Most will do well in containers. Annuals are a natural option, since they last only one season. Flowering bulbs, perennials, ornamental grasses, shrubs, and small trees all adapt well to life in a container. Succulents are especially good specimens for container gardens (and for houseplants; see page 272). Growing herbs and crops like strawberries, tomatoes, and peppers in pots is also ideal for small-space gardening. For hanging baskets, consider easy-to-care-for rhipsalis, sedums, senecios, and ferns, all of which require less maintenance than the usual flowering annuals.

> ▶ **MARTHA GARDENS**
> I love growing dramatic choices like sago palms, begonias, hibiscus (shown opposite), and other tropicals and subtropicals that can be brought indoors during winter. A couple of lessons I've learned from my love affair with tropicals is that each genus of plant is typically extremely large and that the types of plants within the genus are extremely diverse. If you are contemplating a collection, it is essential to keep in mind the space you have available and the size of the plants you desire. That said, many tropical plants do come in smaller varieties, so you really can enjoy tropicals on any scale.

**Select the pots.** For best results, use only containers with drainage holes—waterlogged soil is fatal to almost all potted plants. When purchasing new pots, think about how they will look when staged as a group. Having vessels in a range of shapes, sizes, and materials will produce a more interesting scene than a homogeneous set. Consider whether you will be moving the potted plant inside and out over time; if so, opt for lightweight colored resin or fiberglass pots, which have the appearance of heavier stone or terra-cotta. Likewise, if the container will hold a plant that is hardy enough to remain outside in an area with frigid winters, make sure it, too, can withstand the below-freezing temperatures.

**Prepare the containers.** You will need a sterile, soilless potting mix, sold at garden supply shops. Or you can make your own by blending 2 gallons of coconut coir with 1 gallon each of vermiculite, perlite, compost, and granular fertilizer. Pick a pot whose diameter is about an inch larger than the plant's root mass. Cover the drainage hole in the bottom of the pot with a piece of landscape fabric or a small shard of terra-cotta to prevent the mix from falling out. Then firmly press 1 inch of the mix into the bottom of the pot.

**Pot the plant.** First, place the plants in their designated spots and position them in the order that looks best. Moisten the potting mix before adding it to the pot; it should hold together and crumble loosely when touched. Then fill the pot about two-thirds of the way with the mix. Loosen the roots of the plant with a hori hori, and center the plant in the pot. Place the mix around the root mass, and gently firm it down with your fingers to eliminate air pockets. The plant's crown should be even with the soil level and about 1 inch below the pot's rim. Water the plant until it starts to drain through the holes.

**Feed the plants.** Container plants require extra attention to thrive. Unlike in-ground plants, those in pots have fewer nutrients to draw on because of the limited amount of soil. Add a slow-release fertilizer 2 months after planting and repeatedly during the growing season as instructed on the label.

**Water regularly.** Container plants also require more frequent watering. The plant is thirsty when the soil feels dry an inch below the surface—never let the soil fully dry out. Add enough water so that the water starts to drain through the pot's holes, but don't overdo it (or you'll also drain out nutrients). Don't allow plants to sit in water; empty their saucers after each watering and rainfall, or rest the pots on stands. Another option is what's called bottom watering, whereby you place the potted plant in a tub or sink. Fill it with water halfway up the side of the pot. Water will wick up into the mix through the drainage hole in the pot's bottom. (This method doesn't work for pots filled with bubble wrap or other materials that would prevent the uptake of water from below.) Check the soil surface for moisture. It should not take more than half an hour to saturate the mix. Remove the pot from its bath, and allow excess water to drain out the bottom.

**Maintain the plants.** Some flowering plants require deadheading to encourage new growth (as noted on the plant label). Pinch or snip off dead blooms throughout the season. Those that are covered in small flowers, or that begin to wilt in late summer, should be cut back to one-third the size when the blooms are spent; don't worry, the plant will quickly grow back. When plants outgrow a pot, move them to a pot just one size larger. Be careful of "overpotting"—setting a plant into a pot much larger than the root mass—as this will traumatize or even kill it.

# 11

# GROW YOUR OWN VEGETABLES

There are so many excellent reasons to establish a garden dedicated to growing vegetables, starting with the incomparable flavor of a just-picked carrot or head of lettuce. For many people, especially those who enjoy preparing their meals from scratch, this is reason enough to embark on such a project. Once you have laid the groundwork, a vegetable garden is economical, saving you a significant amount of money in food costs. It also allows you to enjoy varieties that are not found in any grocery store or even at a local farmers' market. Whatever your motivation to embrace this ancient form of backyard homesteading, you can tap into my decades of experience in designing, planting, nurturing, and harvesting productive vegetable gardens.

**Grow what you eat.** Growing vegetables, while not terribly difficult, does require time and effort, so the goal is to focus on the produce you actually enjoy and would otherwise be buying. Besides common varieties, it's worth exploring all the wonderful heirloom varieties that are available in seed form. One way to approach your wish list is to imagine filling your salad bowl with your favorite components, such as different lettuces and leafy greens and whatever else you like to layer in for contrasting crunch and color. Most vegetables are annuals, but perennial plants, such as asparagus, rhubarb, garlic chives, and artichokes, can be planted once and will keep producing.

> ▶ **MARTHA GARDENS**
> What I discovered by growing my own was that fresh-picked asparagus is so much better than anything I had ever had before. So, of course, when I moved to Bedford, I planted several hundred crowns. Since then, eager to try the new hybrids, I have added many varieties, including some purple types, which are pretty in the garden and turn green when cooked. Once the picking season is over, after about 4 weeks, I allow the "ferns" to grow high and thick—up to 6 feet tall. These beautiful ferns are important because they provide rich nutrients to the roots for the next season's growth. In late autumn, the ferns, once softened and ripened by frost, can be cut off at ground level, leaving a clean bed for the following spring. I encourage everyone to plant a few crowns from one of these new hybrids and establish an asparagus garden that will keep producing for many, many years.

**Consider companion planting.** This time-honored strategy involves growing certain crops together for mutual benefits like pest deterrence, improved pollination, better soil health, enhanced flavor, and higher yields—while avoiding incompatible pairs (namely, tomatoes and other nightshades; carrots and parsnip; and fennel with most other vegetables) that compete or attract shared pests. Common examples of favorable pairings include the "three sisters"—corn, squash, and beans—as well as tomatoes and basil, marigolds, nasturtiums, or carrots. Flowers like zinnias, cosmos, and lavender attract pollinators and repel pests, as do sunflowers, which also provide shade for tender lettuces.

**Pick the spot.** Be sure to choose a level location that receives at least 6 to 8 hours of direct sunlight a day. It helps to site it within a garden hose's reach of your outdoor spigot, or you'll need to come up with an irrigation method. Not to be overlooked is having a garden close to your house, when you will be more inclined to enjoy it daily; one that is too far away can be prone to neglect.

**Prepare the site.** If you are converting an existing lawn to a vegetable garden, you will need to remove all grass and weeds from the area. The quickest way to accomplish this is by using a rototiller that pulls up the top layer of sod; alternatively, you can work in sections using a spade and shovel.

**Choose the method.** In-ground rows are a budget-friendly option since no other materials are required, though you will most likely need to take extra steps to improve the existing soil. Most vegetables prefer a slightly acidic soil (pH 6 to 6.8); perform a pH test (as described on page 224) to see what, if any, amendments are needed. The soil should also be loamy, well draining, and rich in nutrients, which is best achieved by working plenty of compost into the rows. Raised beds offer more flexibility and control over the growing environment because they are typically filled with an optimal blend of soil. You can make this yourself using topsoil, compost, and perlite or vermiculite to enhance aeration and drainage, or buy a high-quality organic blend designed for raised-bed gardening from a garden supply center.

**Map it out.** Sketch the garden design to scale, noting what you plant in each in-ground row or raised bed. Account for succession plantings, replacing early and mid-season crops with late-summer and fall vegetables. Note when your vegetables are predicted to reach maturity, and how to tell when they are ready for harvesting. As the season progresses, note what is doing well and what isn't and any possible factors, such as plants that might not be getting enough sun. This will become your guide for proper crop rotation, in particular moving tomatoes and other nightshades to a different spot each year.

**Thin as needed.** When planting from seed, you'll need to thin the plants as directed on the packet. Some (many) gardeners choose to skip this step, but doing so can hinder the ability of any one seedling to take hold.

**Provide steady, even watering.** A general rule of thumb is to water deeply once a week, or more often as needed in dry, hot climates. Direct the water at the roots rather than spraying from above. As always, watering in the morning helps prevent leaf damage, as the gentler morning sunshine evaporates any water that gets on the foliage without drying out the soil.

**Stay on top of weeds.** Weeds will compete for water and nutrients, so be especially proactive about pulling them up early on, when seedlings are getting established, and stay on top of weeding throughout the season. Adding a 3- to 4-inch layer of mulch will help deter weeds and retain soil moisture.

**Feed the soil.** Top-dressing your rows and beds with compost at planting time will get your plants off to a good start. Once the seedlings appear in earnest, begin applying an organic fertilizer as directed on the label, sweeping away any mulch around the plant. You can also continue to side-dress the plants with compost. To promote the production of fruiting plants, such as tomatoes, peppers, melons, cucumbers, and squashes, regularly snip off the stems that are putting out only leaves. This will direct their energy toward those bearing fruit.

**Know how to spot issues.** Check the foliage frequently for any signs of disease and remove infected (usually yellowed) leaves right away. Severely affected plants should be pulled up entirely and destroyed before they infect nearby plants. Be on the lookout as well for common pests that are particularly attracted to vegetable gardens—namely, slugs and snails, tomato hornworms, cabbage white butterflies, and flea, potato, and Japanese beetles. Signs of these invaders include leaves with nibbled-away holes or browned edges, as well as a general loss of foliage. Try banishing them with horticultural oils and soaps rather than chemical pesticides. If those efforts fail, consult with a staff member at a local nursery for guidance.

> ▶ **MARTHA GARDENS**
> I always grow plenty of my three favorite vegetables—spinach, cucumbers, and celery—as well as parsley and mint to use in making my green juice, which I enjoy every single morning. After harvesting, the spinach goes right into my kitchen sink to be washed and dried. The other ingredients include a fruit and a chunk of fresh ginger. I do not peel anything but the fruit, but I do wash everything before using. This would cost you more than ten dollars per serving to buy the fresh juice, as opposed to growing the components yourself.

**Harvest your crops.** Odds are, if you have planted crops that mature at different times, there will be something ready to be harvested every day. The peak window is limited, with certain produce going from perfectly ripe (or underripe) to spoiled in a very short time. Follow the suggested guidelines for harvesting each plant. For example, "cut-and-come" lettuces can be cut within an inch of the base for another head to grow back; others can be pulled entirely out of the ground and the seeds replanted. For a continual harvest of these and other leafy greens, you can pull off some of the outer leaves at a time.

**Preserve the harvest.** Consider ways to avoid letting an abundant supply of end-of-season crops go to waste. The traditional canning method is admittedly time-consuming, but there are easier alternatives that don't require any special equipment. Most vegetables can be quick-pickled, a process that doesn't require any special equipment. Experiment with different combinations and seasonings to see what you like best. (The jars will keep in the refrigerator for up to a month.) Herbs can be air-dried, frozen, or used to make a variety of pestos for keeping in the freezer. Tomatoes can be oven-dried or cooked in a big-batch sauce and then portioned into smaller containers for freezing.

> ▸ **MARTHA GARDENS**
>
> I have a special pickling mix for the smaller turnips I grow from seeds I brought back from Tokyo. The mix is made with Japanese rice wine vinegar, plus a little sugar and salt added in equal amounts. Slice the turnips paper-thin, put them in a jar, and pour the mix over them. Screw on the lid and refrigerate for 2 to 3 days before using. They'll keep for up to a month, refrigerated.

**Extend the growing season.** Unless you live in an area with mild-enough winter climates (such as Hawaii, Southern California, and some parts of the American Southeast and Southwest), the growing season can be pretty limited. Instead of putting away your implements in the fall, a greenhouse enables you to continue to grow—and enjoy!—many types of plants throughout the year. Other less involved and more affordable options include row covers or hoop houses.

> ▸ **MARTHA GARDENS**
>
> I had always grown my own vegetables and had extended the season as much as I could by using cold frames, polytunnels or hoop houses, and deep mulches. But growing certainly slowed; quantities dwindled in January, February, and March, and there was very little to cook. I made up my mind to build a glass greenhouse (opposite) that would allow me to have a steady supply of vegetables year-round, and I'm so pleased with the results. When growing indoors, there are many factors to take into consideration: What are your expectations? What do you want in the way of variety of vegetables? Can you harvest enough of what you want in a confined indoor space? Before I built my greenhouse, I made my lists, and I studied many seed catalogs, searching for varieties that are recommended for greenhouse culture. And I consulted with friends who have had great success. Now my greenhouse is well established. Each morning, I pay it a visit to see how things are thriving and to know what should be harvested or replanted. It is one of the most pleasant things I do, and I get such joy from picking a handful of carrots or bunches of fresh herbs or ripe red tomatoes for a salad.

# 12

# GROW SEASON-LONG CUTTING FLOWERS

Cultivating a cutting-flower garden allows you to grace your home—or those of your friends and family—with beautiful blooms. Annuals, perennials, and bulbs are the most common options, though even ornamental grasses can be used to make distinctive arrangements.

**Choose the site.** Most flowers need 6 to 8 hours of direct sunlight daily and rich, loamy, well-draining soil. If planting in the ground, make sure to work in lots of organic matter. Provide ample space between rows or beds (preferably 2 to 3 feet) for easy harvesting. The spot need not be large, as the plants can be packed tightly for a higher yield (and to crowd weeds out), a practice called intensive planting. You can also incorporate trellises or other structures for climbing roses or clematis.

**Pick plants that can be used for arrangements.** Consider a mix of colors, shapes, sizes, and textures, which will create the most striking bouquets. To make it even more eye-catching, add some foliage plants, such as hostas, as well as ferns and ornamental grasses.

**Stretch the season.** Opt for a variety of plants that will provide blooms from early spring through summer and even into autumn. For example, the garden could come alive with ranunculus, daffodils, and tulips in April before the peonies emerge in mid-May, followed by cosmos, lilies, zinnias, sunflowers, anemones, and dahlias, the latter of which will last until the first frost.

**Focus on peonies.** Despite their short blooming period, these beauties are hardy and undemanding. Herbaceous peony types range from elegant simples, with as few as five petals, to lush doubles, with hundreds. The fewer the petals, the less rainwater the flower absorbs, and the less likely it is to flop over. Space plants 3 to 4 feet apart and away from competing tree roots. Established plants need only regular watering and a single annual application of low-nitrogen fertilizer. Stake as needed during the growing season, using peony rings or other supports. Tree peonies (shown opposite, at Turkey Hill), however, don't require staking, as they grow on woody stems—though choose their location smartly as they can grow 4 to 7 feet tall and 3 to 5 feet wide. Remove spent blooms immediately, before they turn brown and become unsightly. Wait to cut back the foliage (to the ground) until the first frost.

**Explore lilies.** Lilies have one of the longest in-vase lifespans of any cut bloom, and the flowers will continue to mature after they've been cut. They like to have their "head in the sun, feet in the shade," and should be planted where the foliage can get at least 6 hours of full sun per day. Over time, most lilies will multiply, and the plants will grow into large clumps with many stems; fortunately, they don't mind being crowded. As the blossoms begin to fade, snip them off to keep the plants looking neat and tidy. When all the flowers are spent, remove the entire cluster, leaving the stems in place until they turn yellow in late summer or fall. Then cut the stems back to within a couple of inches of the soil surface.

> **▶ MARTHA GARDENS**
> Before bringing cut lilies indoors, gently pull the pollen-holding anthers off each flower to prevent the pollen from getting on the delicate flower petals and shortening their bloom time. When doing this, it's a good idea to wear gloves and clothes you don't mind getting dirty—their pollen is notorious for staining flesh and fabric. If you happen to get a pollen stain on your clothing, do not rub! Instead, reach for a roll of tape and use the sticky side to dab the area gently—the particles will adhere to the tape.

**Incorporate dahlias.** It's worth growing dahlias in your garden for their late-season interest; they add much-needed color to the garden in the hotter months when most other blooming plants are spent. However, their beauty and seemingly endless variety are other reasons to fall in love with dahlias, which look positively stunning in arrangements. (See page 264 for how to care for them.) Some gardeners devote their entire cutting-flower plot to these fan favorites.

**Plant the selection.** Plant each variety in masses so you can quickly gather the desired elements of your arrangements; you may also want to plant in color-coordinated rows. Grow taller varieties behind shorter ones, for easier clipping. Provide the necessary stakes for peonies, dahlias, and other top-heavy plants. All but dahlias should be watered when planted (wait to water those until the first shoots appear).

**Nurture the plants.** Water them deeply once a week, twice during hot, dry spells. Most flowers are heavy feeders; fertilize the soil in the spring and fall and every month during the growing season (or as directed on the seed packet or plant label). Deadheading spent flowers will promote continued blooming. Check frequently for signs of pests and disease, which can spread rapidly in cases of intensive planting.

**Harvest the flowers.** Pick them in the early morning or at dusk when it's cool; avoid harvesting when the flowers are wet from rain or watering. Cut the flowers at a sharp angle, using sharp floral shears or a florist knife for tender stems and secateurs for woody stems. As you go, strip the leaves from the bottom portion of the stems into one bucket, then shake the stems to remove excess dirt and put them in a bucket of water.

# Dahlias

I grow multiple varieties of dahlias, planting three to five of each type, and adding new ones to the collection each growing season. Here are some other pointers for growing and harvesting dahlias.

# Secrets to Success

▶ **TYPES**

Aim for a mix of styles, including pompons, single flower, double flower, cactus, and dinner plate.

▶ **SUNLIGHT**

These heat-loving plants should be planted in a location that receives at least 8 hours of full sun per day.

▶ **DRAINAGE**

It's also essential to provide them with good drainage. Dahlias grow from tubers and can easily rot in wet, poorly draining soil. Make sure the soil is loose and amended with plenty of organic matter. Adding a bit of sand to the soil can also help.

▶ **STAKING**

Because dahlias grow very fast, they will get tall and flop before you realize it, making them ideal for staking. The best time to do this is before they even start growing. When planting your tubers, pound a stake into the ground next to them (you can always add a second one later if needed).

▶ **PINCHING**

Pinching the growing tips or side shoots occasionally is beneficial for certain varieties of dahlias, keeping the plants compact and sturdy as they mature. It also greatly helps to reduce the floppiness of the plants—and as a bonus, more pinching means bushier plants that will put out more blooms.

▶ **DEADHEADING**

Deadheading dahlias not only helps the plant look tidier, it also prevents it from producing seed, stimulating it to make more buds and, thus, more flowers. Continually deadheading them will prolong their blooming season.

▶ **WATERING**

Less is more with dahlias; it is better to underwater than to overwater. Wait until your dahlias just barely start to wilt and are a bit limp between waterings. To prevent mildew or fungus in wet, humid weather, water dahlias from below instead of from above.

▶ **HARVESTING**

Harvest dahlias when they are almost fully open, placing them in cool water right away. The more you harvest, the more blooms the plants will produce. Let them rest out of the sun for a few hours before arranging.

▶ **WINTERIZING**

If you live in an area with frigid winters, you will need to protect your dahlia tubers from the elements. The usual method is to dig them up after their flowers have faded and before the first frost, cleaning and drying them thoroughly before storing in crumpled newspaper inside a shoebox in a cool, dark, dry space. Recently, we've been leaving them in the ground, covering completely with hay, a tarp to shield from rain and snow, and finally a layer of compost and mulch, which can be raked away in late spring. This way, the dahlias begin blooming in June rather than having to wait until August.

Textured greens—feathery peppergrass, spiky datura, and peach-stemmed pokeweed—mix in naturally with stunning pink dahlias and cosmos.

# Flower Arranging

Now that you've devoted much time and energy (and likely space) to caring for your cutting-flower garden, you'll want to follow that up by knowing how to care for fresh blooms to create arresting, long-lasting displays. Here's a mini-manual.

## Secrets to Success

▸ **PREP**
Once you bring the flowers inside, refill the harvesting bucket with fresh water, and trim all stems at a 45-degree angle to maximize the surface area, allowing them to easily drink water.

▸ **CONDITION AS NEEDED**
For example, use pruners to cut an X in the ends of woody branches like lilac to enhance water absorption, and keep daffodil stems in water overnight to release toxic calcium oxalate before mixing them with other varieties.

▸ **PREVENT CONTAMINATION**
Always clean the vase or other vessel that will be used for the arrangement, and pluck leaves from stems that would fall below the waterline.

▸ **PROVIDE SUPPORT**
Use a flower frog (preferably one made from reusable metal or ceramic rather than toxic foam), floral tape, or the sturdier stems in your grouping to hold all your elements in place.

▸ **PLAY WITH SCALE AND COLOR**
Nestle in one big leaf, for example, and pick a palette (go monochromatic or high-contrast). Also mix textures, pairing wispy varieties with smooth ones.

▸ **MAKE BOUQUETS LAST**
Add fresh water and remove wilted or discolored blooms and leaves daily. Keep arrangements out of the sun and away from heat sources.

# 13

# PLANT TREES

Trees add beauty, structure, and importance to properties—through seasonal interest (like fall foliage), shade, privacy, and long-term value. They also clean the air, help you breathe, and provide vital habitat and food for wildlife. It's a good idea to plant a new tree near a large, declining, important one before the declining tree dies.

**Choose the trees.** Select trees that are known to thrive in your area, and buy ones that are grown locally if possible. Young, freshly dug, well-grown trees with a 2- to 4-inch caliper (trunk diameter) are excellent candidates for landscape planting rather than mature, large, more expensive specimens.

**Dig the hole.** Trees are long-term investments, so take the necessary steps to set them up for long-term success. Do not rush this process, as a poorly planted tree will always be vulnerable to disease and wind damage. Dig a hole that's at least three times the diameter of the root ball and just deep enough so the root flare will be at or slightly above the soil level. The hole should have sloping sides to encourage root growth.

**Plant correctly.** The process depends on the way the tree was grown. Slide a "ball and burlap" tree into the hole, cut away as much of the wire basket around the root as you can, and push the burlap down to the bottom of the hole. Bare-root trees should be removed from their wrapping, while container-grown trees can be loosened from the pot. It's crucial to loosen the roots, especially for container-grown trees, either by hand or with a hori hori.

**Finish planting.** Amend the dug-out soil with compost before backfilling, and feed young trees with a fertilizer designed for use at planting time. Be sure to water the tree thoroughly to eliminate air pockets, and also several times a week during its first summer. Mulching around the base is also recommended to retain moisture; make sure the mulch does not touch the base of the trunk, to prevent root rot, fungal diseases, and other concerns.

**Water regularly.** Already established trees with strong, deep root systems will be more drought tolerant, but some younger plantings require supplemental watering during the hotter, drier months. Plan on watering to a depth of 6 to 8 inches each time. You can use a soaker hose or drip irrigation to deliver water directly to the root zone, moving the hose or soaker periodically to cover the entire area under the tree's canopy.

> ▸ **MARTHA GARDENS**
> I am a passionate advocate for planting trees, viewing them as essential elements of any landscape, yard, or garden. I have personally planted thousands and thousands of trees on my Bedford farm over the years, including orchards, allées (opposite), woodlands of Japanese maples, and reforestation efforts.

# 14

# NURTURE HOUSEPLANTS

For many people, houseplants are an easy way to bring life indoors, regardless of whether outdoor gardening is an option. With their varied shapes, textures, and colors, they enliven interiors year-round. Creating an indoor garden has also been shown to have physical and mental health benefits, including improving your mood, reducing stress, boosting concentration, and easing dry skin and respiratory ailments. Many houseplants are easy to care for, but they do require more attention than outdoor plants.

**Choose the plants.** Start by understanding your environment—how much light and space you have and matching it up appropriately to the plant's needs and growth habit. There is also a plant for every skill level. Assess how much attention you can devote to them. Succulents, for instance, are notoriously easy to grow, even for beginners; try euphorbias, echeverias, senecios, spider plants, jade plants, and snake plants. Other low-maintenance options include orchids, monsteras, Chinese money plants, and begonias. Be sure to buy plants that are nontoxic to any pets in your home.

**Transplant.** Unless your plant came in an attractive container, you'll want to give it a prettier home. Choose a pot with proper drainage. A soil mix containing components like lava rock, coconut fiber, and sand ensures good drainage. Create a humid environment by placing pots on pebbles in a tray filled with water.

**Provide ample light.** Every plant has its own needs, as indicated on the plant tag. In general, east- or west-facing windows work for sun or part-sun plants, while north-facing windows are suitable for shade lovers.

> **▶ MARTHA GARDENS**
> One of my great pleasures is growing fancy-leaved begonias, a passion that began on my grandmother's sun porch in Buffalo. I especially love rhizomatous varieties for their dramatic leaves, which thrive in bright, indirect light and grow happily in shallow pots. They're long-lived, surprisingly pest-free, and need only modest watering. With a small pair of scissors, I keep them tidy—and with a single leaf, I can propagate a new plant. When properly grown, begonias bring lasting beauty indoors, and I often bring my best specimens—such as the Brazilian beauties, opposite—inside to decorate every room when I entertain.

**Water in moderation.** Water your houseplants well, but don't overdo it. Many houseplants suffer from too much watering, not too little. Test for dampness by sticking your finger into the soil up to your first knuckle. If it's dry, water using the same method experts recommend for gardens and yards: Rather than sprinkling a few drops every day, which keeps roots closer to the surface, pour long, less frequent drinks so they grow deeply. If possible, first move the pots to your sink or tub, and use a long-spouted watering can to direct the stream to the soil until excess water flows out of the drainage hole. Plan to water deeply more often in winter, when homes are filled with dry heat, than in the summertime when the indoor conditions are more humid.

**Feed.** Fertilize the plants regularly (as noted on the plant tag or product label) during the growing season, which for most plants starts in March and ends in November. Fish emulsion is a great all-purpose option; just add some to your watering can once a month.

**Groom.** Keeping plants tidy is about more than aesthetics—it helps them stay healthy, too. Dirt and grime on the leaves hinder photosynthesis, so wipe down the foliage as needed. Snip any dead or yellowing leaves, as they can harbor disease and pests. And hydrate the air, too, especially in winter, since dehydrated plants can attract invaders like spider mites. To increase humidity, fill a metal or plastic tray a few inches deep with pebbles, then add water and put your plants on top. Refill when the liquid evaporates.

**Repot and revive.** When a plant has outgrown its pot, you'll need to transplant it to a bigger vessel. The two signs to look out for are when its roots burst from the pot's drainage hole and when it wilts shortly after being watered. To repot it, choose a slightly larger container and cover the drainage hole loosely with a pottery shard or flat stone; this allows water but not soil to escape. Place a scoop or two of organic potting mix in the bottom. Carefully remove the plant from its old vessel and gently tease out the roots to encourage them to spread. Then, simply lower it into the new pot. The top of the root ball should sit about 1 inch below the rim. Fill in with more potting mix, tamp it down lightly, and water thoroughly.

T

The subjects in this book—cooking, entertaining, home organizing, collecting, and gardening—may seem distinct, but for me they are and always have been inseparable. Together, they form a framework for living thoughtfully and beautifully.

What unites these pursuits—which are central to my own life as well as my business—is that skill is built gradually through repetition and care. The best way to master the subjects is by incorporating them into your daily, weekly, or monthly routines. Practice, in other words, makes progress, helping you feel more confident and capable over time.

Whether stocking the pantry, creating a reliable menu repertoire, maintaining an orderly home, building collections that reflect your personality, or tending a garden and houseplants—these worthwhile activities are deeply rooted in the same discipline: paying attention and doing the work regularly.

Preparation, as you have seen throughout these pages, is a common theme. Reading a recipe all the way through before beginning, planning a meal and table settings, assigning everything a proper place, and drawing a garden on paper before planting are not burdensome steps; they are what allow you to have more time for other pursuits and pastimes.

Prioritizing quality over quantity is another essential theme. Invest thoughtfully—be it in ingredients, cooking and gardening tools, storage systems, or collectibles—and maintain what you have. These choices will save you so much time, money, and effort in the long run while creating surroundings that support rather than distract, both now and in the future.

Finally, remember that all the above is ongoing. The takeaways in each chapter are designed to help you adapt the primary lessons over time. Your cooking routine will change, your hosting skills will expand, your garden will mature, your collections will shift, and your home will experience many transitions. This continuing evolution (particularly when my grandchildren were born) has been deeply rewarding in my own life, providing me with new challenges, new perspectives, and new opportunities for learning and discovery.

If this book (my 102nd!) has done its job, it has not given you rigid rules to follow, but flexible principles to return to again and again. I hope that it encourages you to approach your home—and the life within it—with care, curiosity, and confidence. This way, you can cook, entertain, organize, collect, and garden with ease, efficiency, and enjoyment.

*Martha Stewart*

# ACKNOWLEDGMENTS

I hope this book (my 102nd!) inspires you to master the art of every day.

*The Martha Way* would not have been possible without the collaborative and dedicated team of editorial director Susanne Ruppert, contributing editor Evelyn Battaglia, and designer James Maikowski. Sarah Carey was kind enough to offer her considerable cooking knowledge.

Over the years, our Martha Stewart colleagues have devoted themselves to the subjects featured in this book—cooking, entertaining, home organizing, collecting, and gardening—to keep our readers informed. Thank you to each and every one, particularly Kevin Sharkey, Thomas Joseph, Ryan McCallister, Darcy Miller, Hannah Milman, Lucinda Scala Quinn, Jennifer Aaronson, Fritz Karch, Margaret Roach, and Anthony Santelli.

We have been fortunate to work with many talented photographers. Thank you to those whose beautiful work graces these pages (for a full list, see page 281), notably Chelsea Cavanaugh, Dana Gallagher, Bryan Gardner, Marcus Nilsson, José Picayo, and Yasu+Junko. Kim Dumer generously provided her expertise regarding photo rights.

Instrumental with their continuing support are Susan Magrino and her team, Heather Kirkland, Ryan Mesina, Judy Morris, Sophie Roche, and Jocelyn Santos.

We are pleased to be making books with our Harvest/HarperCollins family, namely Diana Baroni, Tai Blanche, Yeon Kim, Mumtaz Mustafa, Shelby Peak, Rachel Meyers, and Jacqueline Quirk.

# ▶ PHOTOGRAPHY CREDITS

**Sang An** 182, 184–85

**Burcu Avsar** 180 *(right)*

**Christopher Baker** 3, 103, 233, 234, 237

**Roland Bello** 202–203

**Fadil Berisha** 117

**Marion Brenner** 260

**Anita Calero** 99, 191 *(4)*, 279

**Chelsea Cavanaugh** 166, 176, 179 *(right)*, 193 *(left)*, 194 *(2)*, 195

**Elizabeth Cecil** 45

**Christopher Churchill** 5

**Samantha Contis** 227, 238, 251, 270–271

**Paul Costello** 167 *(right)*, 246

**Craig Cutler** 205, 207 *(left)*

**Joseph De Leo** 180 *(left)*

**Victor Demarchelier** 2, 109, 148, 265

**Noe Dewitt** 7 *(potted plants)*, 78, 97

**John Dolan** 214

**Pieter Estersohn** 58

**Frank Frances** 135

**Dana Gallagher** 31, 55, 67, 68, 76, 92, 136, 156, 168 *(left)*, 208, 218–219

**Bryan Gardner** 7 *(place setting)*, 41, 72, 104–105, 169, 179 *(left)*, 207 *(right)*

**Gentl & Hyers** 25

**Hans Gissinger** 46 *(sautéing)*

**John Gruen** 255

**Louise Hagger** 15, 266

**Murray Hall** 10, 187, 198, 256

**Gabriela Herman** 221, 252, 262–263, 269

**Jenny Huang** 53

**Lisa Hubbard** 100, 259

**Ditte Isager** 20

**John Kernick** 116

**Mike Krautter** 47 *(steaming)*

**Frédéric Lagrange** 106, 228

**Ryan Liebe** 23, 42, 47 *(poaching and parchment)*

**Thomas Loof** 91

**David Malosh** 33, 87, 95

**Charles Maraia** 57, 139, 147

**Kate Mathis** 125, 141

**Johnny Miller** 6, 113, 114, 118, 144, 206, 217, 231

**Karen Mordechai** 93, 96

**Ngoc Minh Ngo** 115, 273

**Marcus Nilsson** 24, 38, 46 *(slow-roasting)*, 88–89, 111, 132, 197

**Victoria Pearson** 155

**José Picayo** 4, 161, 162, 164, 165, 167 *(left)*, 174, 213

**Con Poulos** 27, 28, 71, 75

**Linda Pugliese** 123

**Courtesy of Revman** 7 *(Martha Stewart bedding)*

**Maria Robledo** 85, 190, 225, 245

**Lisa Romerein** 128

**Annie Schlechter** 288

**Victor Schrager** 188

**Christopher Simpson** 34

**Celeste Sloman** 127

**Michael Scott Slosar** 242

**Seth Smooth** 83

**Claire Takacs** 241

**Dane Tashima** 280

**Christopher Testani** 62, 63 *(process shots)*

**Martyn Thompson** 200, 201

**Jonny Valiant** 172, 274

**Mikkel Vang** 64

**Justin Walker** 19

**Björn Wallander** 84, 248

**Lennart Weibull** 16, 49, 50, 61

**Matthew Williams** 131

**Yasu + Junko** 7 *(spoons)*, 168 *(right)*, 171, 177 *(2)*, 178, 181, 192, 193 *(right)*

# ► INDEX

## A

air-conditioning units, changing filters, 146
air purifiers, 149
alcoholic-free beverages, 97
ale pitchers, 200
amaranth, 36
ambiance, creating inviting, 102–7
animal-shaped ceramics, 194
antique fairs, 204
antiques. *See also* collecting
shopping, 170, 173, 204
artichokes, 250
prepping, 29
asparagus, 30, 250
attics
organizing, 152
safety, 153

## B

Bakelite, 163, 173, 177
baking, 56, 59
collectibles, 206–7
desserts recipes, 66–77
pâte brisée, 62–63
staples, 56
substitutions, 60
tools, 56
baking powder/soda, 56, 59, 60
balloon whisks, 21
ballpoint ink, stain removal, 151
barley, 36
barware, 82, 94
collectibles, 170, 178–79
washing, 82
baseboards, 143
basements
cleaning, 154
organizing, 152
safety, 154
baskets, for storage and organizing, 13, 122, 124, 129, 130
bathmats, 142
bathrooms
cleaning, 138, 140, 142
guests and parties, 107, 115
organizing, 122, 124, 134

bath towels, 134, 142
bathtubs, 142, 143
bedding
cleaning, 142, 146, 149
hosting guests, 115
Bedford farm, 110, 122, 159, 170, 199
gardens, 173, 210, 212, 223, 247, 250, 268
bedrooms
hosting guests, 115
organizing, 133
beds
making, 140
organizing underneath, 124
beer, 97, 101
begonias, 272
belongings, paring down, 122
best-by dates, 59
beverages, 81, 94–97
glassware for. *See* glassware
beverage servers, 85
bills. *See* paperwork; tax documents
blanching, 29
blankets, 115
blenders, 21
books
collecting, 158, 173
gardening, 158, 211, 212
organizing and cleaning, 124, 126, 138, 145
preventing warping, 145, 196
bottle openers, 94, 178
brass objects, 175
breading, 35, 39
Brownies, 69
brown rice, 36
brown sugar, 56, 60
bubble bud vases, 193
buckwheat, 36
buffets, 90
bulbs, planting, 232–35
bulgur, 36
butter dishes, 160, 169
buttermilk, 60

## C

cabbage, 30
presenting dips and spreads in head of, 89
cabinets. *See* kitchen cabinets; medicine cabinets
caipirinhas, 94
cake flour, 60
cakes
New York Cheesecake, 73
One-Bowl Chocolate Layer Cake, 77
Pound Cake, 70
cake stands, 90, 207
calendars. *See* schedules
cameos, 177
candles, 101, 107
canning, 257
capers, 52
carbon monoxide detectors, 154
car, cleaning out, 138
carpets, 146
carrots, 22, 30
gardening, 253
prepping, 29
cast-iron skillets, 21
catalogs, 138, 142
ceilings, cleaning, 145
celery, 22, 30, 254
celery glasses, 193
centerpieces, 101, 102
ceramic pie birds, 166, 206
champagne flutes/coupes, 82, 181, 183
Cheesecake, New York, 73
chicken
breading, 35, 39
roasted, 35, 40
stock, 22
children, entertaining tips, 110
chimney inspections, 154
Chocolate Chip Cookies, 66
Chocolate Layer Cake, One-Bowl, 77
chocolate, stain removal, 150
cider, 110
citrus peelers, 94
cleaning, 140–49
developing maintenance mindset, 152–53
for entertaining, 98
general principles for, 146, 149
guest rooms, 115

hosting, 81, 108. *See also* entertaining
    beverages, 94
    essentials, 82, 85
    gifts for hosts, 81, 108
    holiday brunches, 90
    houseguests, 112–16
houseguests, 112–16
    gifts for host, 81, 108
houseplants, 272, 275
HVAC, 146, 153, 154

# I

ice buckets, 94, 177
ice cream, 93
ice-cube molds, 94
ink, stain removal, 151
intensive planting, 258, 261
introductory tours, 116
inventory, pantry, 22, 24
ironing, 124

# J

jadeite, 167
jiggers, 94, 178
junk drawers, 126

# K

kamut, 37
Kew Royal Botanic Gardens, 158
kimono trays, 170
kitchen. *See also* cooking
    cleaning, 140, 145
    collectibles, 166–69
    equipment, 18–21
    establishing good habits in, 48–52
    organizing, 121, 122, 126, 129
kitchen cabinets
    cleaning, 142, 145
    organizing, 126, 129, 138
kitchen drain, 142
kitchen islands, 122, 126
kitchen labels, 130
kitchen scraps, 22, 51, 222

kitchen sinks
    cleaning, 48, 98, 142
    under area, 134
knife sharpeners, 18
knives, 18
    sharpening, 18
    using, 26
kosher salt, 52

# L

labeling, 130, 153, 196
laundry rooms, organizing, 124, 130
lavender seeds, 173
lawn games, 110
leaks, 146, 153
leather furniture, 145
leftovers, 51
lighting, 142
like with like. *See* grouping principles
lilies, 261
linen closets, 124
linens. *See* bedding
lipstick, stain removal, 151
lunch boxes, 194

# M

magazines, 116, 138, 142
mail, sorting, 138
maintenance mindset, 152–53
    seasonal checklists, 154
makeup
    organizing, 138, 145
    stain removal, 151
makeup compacts, 176
mangoes, 14, 17
Martha-tinis, 94
mattresses, 145
mattress pads, 143
measuring ingredients, 48
meat mallets, 21
medicine cabinets, 134, 143
menu planning, 86, 90, 98
Microplane graters, 21
millet, 37
mirrors, 134, 142
mise en place, 48
mocktails, 97

monthly deep cleanings, 143
mortars and pestles, 126
mud, stain removal, 151
mulch (mulching), 224, 235, 239, 243, 254, 268
multitaskers, 137
multitasking spaces, 124
music playlists, 107
mussels, 86
mustard, stain removal, 151

# N

napkins, 85, 98, 102
New York Botanical Gardens, 158
New York Cheesecake, 73
New York strip, 44
nightstands, 138
Nishiki Market (Kyoto), 170
no-shoe policy, 146
nurseries, 215, 226

# O

oats, 37
odd number of items, 186
omelets, 35
One-Bowl Chocolate Layer Cake, 77
onions, 30
    chopping, 26
    substitutions, 52
organizing
    about, 120–21
    for entertaining, 98–101
    home. *See* home organizing
ovens, cleaning, 142, 145
oven temperature, 51
"overpotting," 249

# P

pan gravy, 40
pantry
    cleaning, 142, 145
    reorganizing, 138
    stocking, 22–25, 112
    streamlining, 129
    taking inventory, 25, 129